Marcia Hill
Editor

More than a Mirror: How Clients Influence Therapists' Lives

Harrington Park Press

More than a Mirror: How Clients Influence Therapists' Lives

More than a Mirror:
How Clients Influence
Therapists' Lives

Marcia Hill, EdD
Editor

More than a Mirror: How Clients Influence Therapists' Lives, edited by Marcia Hill, was simultaneously issued by The Haworth Press, Inc., under the same title, as a special issue of the journal *Women & Therapy,* Volume 20, Number 1 1997, Marcia Hill and Esther D. Rothblum, Co-Editors.

Harrington Park Press
An Imprint of
The Haworth Press, Inc.
New York • London

Published by

Harrington Park Press, 10 Alice Street, Binghamton, NY 13904-1580 USA

Harrington Park Press is an imprint of The Haworth Press, Inc., 10 Alice Street, Binghamton, NY 13904-1580 USA.

More than a Mirror: How Clients Influence Therapists' Lives has also been published as *Women & Therapy*, Volume 20, Number 1 1997.

The development, preparation, and publication of this work has been undertaken with great care. However, the publisher, employees, editors, and agents of The Haworth Press and all imprints of The Haworth Press, Inc., including The Haworth Medical Press and Pharmaceutical Products Press, are not responsible for any errors contained herein or for consequences that may ensue from use of materials or information contained in this work. Opinions expressed by the author(s) are not necessarily those of The Haworth Press, Inc.

Library of Congress Cataloging-in-Publication Data

More than a mirror : how clients influence therapists' lives / Marcia Hill, editor.
    p. cm.
   Includes bibliographical references and index.
   ISBN 1-56023-099-1 (alk. paper)–ISBN 1-56023-251-X (pbk.)
   1. Psychotherapist and patient. 2. Psychotherapists–Psychology. 3. Countertransference (Psychology) I. Hill, Marcia.
RC480.8.M67 1997
616.89′14–dc21
                      97-6349
                      CIP

INDEXING & ABSTRACTING

Contributions to this publication are selectively indexed or abstracted in print, electronic, online, or CD-ROM version(s) of the reference tools and information services listed below. This list is current as of the copyright date of this publication. See the end of this section for additional notes.

- *Abstracts of Research in Pastoral Care & Counseling*, Loyola College, 7135 Minstrel Way, Suite 101, Columbia, MD 21045

- *Academic Abstracts/CD-ROM,* EBSCO Publishing Editorial Department, P.O. Box 590, Ipswich, MA 01938-0590

- *Academic Index (on-line)*, Information Access Company, 362 Lakeside Drive, Foster City, CA 94404

- *Alternative Press Index*, Alternative Press Center, Inc., P.O. Box 33109, Baltimore, MD 21218-0401

- *Behavioral Medicine Abstracts*, University of Washington, School of Social Work, Seattle, WA 98195

- *CNPIEC Reference Guide: Chinese National Directory of Foreign Periodicals*, P.O. Box 88, Beijing, People's Republic of China

- *Current Contents: Clinical Medicine/Life Sciences (CC: CM/LS) (weekly Table of Contents Service), and Social Science Citation Index. Articles also searchable through Social SciSearch, ISI's online database and in ISI's Research Alert current awareness service*, Institute for Scientific Information, 3501 Market Street, Philadelphia, PA 19104-3302 (USA)

- *Digest of Neurology and Psychiatry,* The Institute of Living, 400 Washington Street, Hartford, CT 06106

- *Expanded Academic Index,* Information Access Company, 362 Lakeside Drive, Forest City, CA 94404

- *Family Studies Database (online and CD/ROM),* National Information Services Corporation, 306 East Baltimore Pike, 2nd Floor, Media, PA 19063

- *Family Violence Research*, Family Violence & Sexual Assault Institute, 1121 E. South East Loop 323, Suite 130, Tyler, TX 75701

- *Feminist Periodicals: A Current Listing of Contents*, Women's Studies Librarian-at-Large, 728 State Street, 430 Memorial Library, Madison, WI 53706

- *Health Source: Indexing & Abstracting of 160 selected health related journals, updated monthly:* EBSCO Publishing, 83 Pine Street, Peabody, MA 01960

(continued)

- *Health Source Plus: expanded version of "Health Source" to be released shortly:* EBSCO Publishing, 83 Pine Street, Peabody, MA 01960
- *Higher Education Abstracts*, Claremont Graduate School, 231 East Tenth Street, Claremont, CA 91711
- *IBZ International Bibliography of Periodical Literature*, Zeller Verlag GmbH & Co., P.O.B. 1949, d-49009, Osnabruck, Germany
- *Index to Periodical Articles Related to Law*, University of Texas, 727 East 26th Street, Austin, TX 78705
- *INTERNET ACCESS (& additional networks) Bulletin Board for Libraries ("BUBL"), coverage of information resources on INTERNET, JANET, and other networks.*
  - JANET X.29: UK.AC.BATH.BUBL or 00006012101300
  - TELNET: BUBL.BATH.AC.UK or 138.38.32.45 login 'bubl'
  - Gopher: BUBL.BATH.AC.UK (138.32.32.45). Port 7070
  - World Wide Web: http: / / www.bubl.bath.ac.uk./BUBL/ home.html
  - NISSWAIS: telnetniss.ac.uk (for the NISS gateway)
  The Andersonian Library, Curran Building, 101 St. James Road, Glasgow G4 ONS, Scotland
- *Mental Health Abstracts (online through DIALOG)*, IFI/Plenum Data Company, 3202 Kirkwood Highway, Wilmington, DE 19808
- *ONS Nursing Scan in Oncology-NAACOG's Women's Health Nursing Scan*, NURSECOM, Inc., 1211 Locust Street, Philadelphia, PA 19107
- *PASCAL International Bibliography T205: Sciences de l'information Documentation*, INIST/CNRS-Service Gestion des Documents Primaires, 2, allee du Parc de Brabois, F-54514 Vandoeuvre-les-Nancy, Cedex, France
- *Periodical Abstracts, Research I* (general & basic reference indexing & abstracting data-base from University Microfilms International (UMI), 300 North Zeeb Road, P.O. Box 1346, Ann Arbor, MI 48106-1346), UMI Data Courier, P.O. Box 32770, Louisville, KY 40232-2770
- *Periodical Abstracts, Research II* (broad coverage indexing & abstracting data-base from University Microfilms International (UMI), 300 North Zeeb Road, P.O. Box 1346, Ann Arbor, MI 48106-1346), UMI Data Courier, P.O. Box 32770, Louisville, KY 40232-2770
- *Psychological Abstracts (PsycINFO)*, American Psychological Association, P.O. Box 91600, Washington, DC 20090-1600
- *Published International Literature on Traumatic Stress (The PILOTS Database)*, National Center for Post-Traumatic Stress Disorder (116 D), VA Medical Center, White River Junction, VT 05009
- *Sage Family Studies Abstracts (SFSA)*, Sage Publications, Inc., 2455 Teller Road, Newbury Park, CA 91320

(continued)

- ***Social Work Abstracts***, National Association of Social Workers, 750 First Street NW, 8th Floor, Washington, DC 20002
- ***Studies on Women Abstracts***, Carfax Publishing Company, P.O. Box 25, Abingdon, Oxfordshire OX14 3UE, United Kingdom
- ***Violence and Abuse Abstracts: A Review of Current Literature on Interpersonal Violence (VAA)***, Sage Publications, Inc., 2455 Teller Road, Newbury Park, CA 91320
- ***Women Studies Abstracts***, Rush Publishing Company, P.O. Box 1, Rush, NY 14543
- ***Women's Studies Index (indexed comprehensively)***, G. K. Hall & Co., 1633 Broadway, 5th Floor, New York, NY 10019

SPECIAL BIBLIOGRAPHIC NOTES

related to special journal issues (separates)
and indexing/abstracting

☐ indexing/abstracting services in this list will also cover material in any "separate" that is co-published simultaneously with Haworth's special thematic journal issue or DocuSerial. Indexing/abstracting usually covers material at the article/chapter level.

☐ monographic co-editions are intended for either non-subscribers or libraries which intend to purchase a second copy for their circulating collections.

☐ monographic co-editions are reported to all jobbers/wholesalers/approval plans. The source journal is listed as the "series" to assist the prevention of duplicate purchasing in the same manner utilized for books-in-series.

☐ to facilitate user/access services all indexing/abstracting services are encouraged to utilize the co-indexing entry note indicated at the bottom of the first page of each article/chapter/contribution.

☐ this is intended to assist a library user of any reference tool (whether print, electronic, online, or CD-ROM) to locate the monographic version if the library has purchased this version but not a subscription to the source journal.

☐ individual articles/chapters in any Haworth publication are also available through the Haworth Document Delivery Services (HDDS).

CONTENTS

ALL HARRINGTON PARK PRESS BOOKS
ARE PRINTED ON CERTIFIED
ACID-FREE PAPER

ABOUT THE EDITOR

Marcia Hill, EdD, is a feminist therapist in private practice in Montpelier, Vermont. She also does consulting, writing, and teaching in the areas of feminist therapy theory and practice. She is a member and past Chair of the Feminist Therapy Institute. Marcia has been involved in grassroots political work for almost 20 years, including helping to start a shelter for battered women. Her free time is spent gardening, backpacking, and maintaining a home in a rural area.

Forewarning

How is it that in all that's written about therapy we so rarely read about the person of the therapist? For a profession whose blood and breath is the unwavering examination of the most personal of human experiences, this omission seems surpassingly strange. It is as if therapy were something that happened to the client only, the therapist a shadowy figure who makes it possible without quite participating.

Therapists do discuss "countertransference," but that experience of being caught in one's own history in response to a client is only one facet of how our clients influence us, perhaps even the smallest facet. There is an increasing body of literature about "vicarious traumatization" (McCann & Pearlman, 1990), the injury to the witness to the recounting of trauma; again, this is only a small part of therapy's impact on the therapist. And there is a range of material about empathy, notably the work of Mahrer (1983), Rogers (1961), and the Stone Center (e.g., Surrey, 1987), although even this is largely depersonalized. Empathy, as any student will tell you, is a tool for affecting the client.

It is not easy to examine how deeply and personally both the practice of therapy and our individual clients influence us as therapists and as people. Therapy is not a one-way process, although the therapist is clearly there in the service of the client and every ethical therapist knows that the client's therapy hour is not the place for the discussion or resolution of her own difficulties. Yet therapy affects the therapist profoundly and irrevocably. Every client moves us emotionally; we learn something from each person. The business of bearing witness to so many lives transforms us as no other work could. We may write and talk about therapy as if it were all about how to impact the client, but all the time we too are being impacted.

[Haworth co-indexing entry note]: "Forewarning." Hill, Marcia. Co-published simultaneously in *Women & Therapy* (The Haworth Press, Inc.) Vol. 20, No. 1, 1997, pp. xxi-xxii; and: *More than a Mirror: How Clients Influence Therapists' Lives* (ed: Marcia Hill) Harrington Park Press, an imprint of The Haworth Press, Inc., 1997, pp. xiii-xiv. Single or multiple copies of this article are available for a fee from The Haworth Document Delivery Service [1-800-342-9678, 9:00 a.m. - 5:00 p.m. (EST). E-mail address: getinfo@haworth.com].

Perhaps every professional license or certification should bear the warning: Your clients will change you. You will be both enriched and injured. You will never be the same: Be forewarned.

Marcia Hill

REFERENCES

Mahrer, A.R. (1983). *Experiential Psychotherapy: Basic Practices.* New York: Brunner/Mazel.

McCann, I.L., & Pearlman, L.A. (1990). Vicarious traumatization: A framework for understanding the psychological effects of working with victims. *Journal of Traumatic Stress, 3,* 131-149.

Rogers, C.R. (1961). *On Becoming a Person.* Boston, MA: Houghton Mifflin.

Surrey, J.L. (1987). Relationship and empowerment. *Work in Progress, 30.* Wellesley, MA: Stone Center Working Papers Series.

My Heart Is Broken by a Five-Year-Old Who "Abandons" Me

Gail Anderson

SUMMARY. This article tells the story of a five-year-old Native American Lakota girl teaching me that I needed to prioritize her agenda in therapy, rather than my own. It was important that I taught her what I could about respecting her own heritage. But what she needed most of all was safety, consistency, nurture and hope as she survived the transition from her birth family to a foster family and to an unknown future. Because the situation called for a big emotional investment in Annie for a time, I felt bereft when my part in her life was over. *[Article copies available for a fee from The Haworth Document Delivery Service: 1-800-342-9678. E-mail address: getinfo@haworth.com]*

Annie was her name. I'd first known of her when she was in her mother's womb. One of her favorite stories was about how well her mother Nell had cared for her in the first three years of her life before Nell's psychosis had surfaced. I had personally witnessed that care because I saw Nell in therapy occasionally at that time and Annie was always with her.

Nell was 14 when I had first seen her; she was 15 when Annie was born. Nell had asked that I see her daughter when Annie was placed in

Gail Anderson is a masters level psychotherapist who works for a non-profit agency, Lutheran Social Service, in rural Minnesota. She specializes in working with children and their families.

Address correspondence to: Gail Anderson, LSS Behavioral Health, 26 7th Avenue North, St. Cloud, MN 56303.

[Haworth co-indexing entry note]: "My Heart Is Broken by a Five-Year-Old Who 'Abandons' Me." Anderson, Gail. Co-published simultaneously in *Women & Therapy* (The Haworth Press, Inc.) Vol. 20, No. 1, 1997, pp. 1-4; and: *More than a Mirror: How Clients Influence Therapists' Lives* (ed: Marcia Hill) Harrington Park Press, an imprint of The Haworth Press, Inc., 1997, pp. 1-4. Single or multiple copies of this article are available for a fee from The Haworth Document Delivery Service [1-800-342-9678, 9:00 a.m. - 5:00 p.m. (EST). E-mail address: getinfo@haworth.com].

1

foster care. My job was to monitor Annie's progress and help her through the difficult and prolonged time when Nell, the tribe and the county were trying to figure out what would happen to Annie and her sisters.

Most often in our therapy time together Annie was a typical five-year-old, busy and happy. She was in a good foster home, the one I'd often said I'd like to live in if I needed one. Her younger sister, Dove, and later, her baby sister, Missy, all lived in the same home.

But some days Annie was sad and really wanted to be rocked and held. We had glowing stars on the ceiling of the playroom and we'd turn off the lights, look at the glow stars and make wishes. "I wish my mom would get well." "I wish my dad and my mom would get back together." Those poignant wishes worked their way into my heart.

More often it appeared Annie needed to distance from her birth parents. I knew when Annie needed to distance because she got bossy. She would test me on boundaries I thought we had established much earlier. I tried to get her to look at what the feelings were behind the bossiness and I reasserted the boundaries. But it wasn't hard to understand that Annie needed a feeling of being in control. There were times when, as her advocate, I faced the complexity of Annie's world and mirrored Annie's feelings of desperately wanting some order in the chaos.

Annie had other challenges. Although Annie was Lakota via both parents, Annie had lived all her five years in a primarily white culture in a small, rural town. While two reservations were within an hour's drive, Annie had not been to either one. She preferred to play with white dolls, rather than the Native American dolls. Further, Annie lived in a white foster home. She had been briefly placed with a Lakota family, but that placement had ended abruptly with a family crisis and there wasn't another Native American family available.

Initially I had struggled about whether I should see Annie in play therapy at all. The difference between who she needed and who I was seemed perfectly clear. It would have been so much more powerful for her therapist to be Native herself, to model pride in heritage, to mirror Annie's shiny black hair, deep brown eyes, sepia skin, regional Lakota speech pattern, the strong Lakota value system and the myriad subtle connections two persons from a similar identified culture share. How I regretted that there was no Native American therapist for children in the area.

What capacity did I have as a member of the "dominant" Anglo-European culture to work competently with a child whose ethnicity is depicted as minority within this culture, even though that child's ancestors were among the first families who lived on this continent? Annie's internalized oppression was revealed by her preference for white dolls, her hurt when someone called her "Indian" and her embarrassment that her Native American mother was mentally ill and her Native American father was chemically dependent. Her relatives, with whom she had some contact, were mostly poor and struggling; many were chemically dependent. She needed to know that there were many different kinds of Native Americans, I told myself. She needed to understand the part racism had played in her family's story. I thought about how strongly I believe women should have the choice of a woman therapist. I worked myself up into quite a self-centered frenzy about who I wasn't.

Despite this mentality, I made attempts to model respect for her heritage as best I could. When we played dolls I waited until Annie had chosen her favorite doll, always white. I then consistently chose a Native American doll whom I identified as my favorite "because she was so smart, loving and beautiful." I would go on to say that my doll looked like Annie. Already Annie did not feel beautiful and would clearly say so. Given her internalized oppression, I was pleased her white doll would even interact with my Native doll! We read books and talked about what being Native American means as well as I could transmit that. We talked about how white people sometimes put Native Americans down, but that it's important to love yourself anyway. These were all appropriate things to do.

However, gradually it dawned on me that Annie's greatest need at this point in her life was consistency and nurture. I had to prioritize Annie's agenda, rather than my own agenda about what I thought Annie's agenda should be. While I continued to include education on Annie's heritage, stories from her culture and stories we made up together, I was freed from my self-created tyranny to be primarily responsible for Annie's education about her heritage and society's racism. I hoped that Annie would have a more competent teacher on anti-racism and cultural pride in the future. But Annie's repetitive and direct message to me was that she needed to act out the story of an intact and untroubled family.

It was more important for me to help Annie understand mental illness, and that her mom being sick was not her fault. She needed to hear that her mom loved her very much and wished she could care for Annie and her sisters herself, and she needed to hear that over and over and over again.

Therapy flowed better at this point. Annie would put me through prescribed rituals each time I saw her. "Call me honey," she instructed. When I got that down, she'd change her request, "Call me sweetie." She would ask, "Put me to bed." She would call me "Mommy"; here was the "daughter" I had never had. I would tuck her into our hastily created nest and she would tell me to turn out the lights. Then we would make up stories about the past, the present and the future. We would play dress-up and make dinner together. What Annie needed was ritual, consistency, nurture and assurance that hope was justified.

When I see a child in therapy who lives with a parent, it is imperative that I never, consciously or unconsciously, compete with the parent for the parental role. Seeing a child who knows she is not "going home" requires a far deeper commitment. It is important to serve as a consistent source of empathy, to model respect for a child's original family and story and to symbolize hope for the future "home." Loving a child in this intense way can be wrenching when therapy is over.

This is the child I wanted to take into my own home and love as my daughter. This is the child who ultimately "abandoned" me for a real home and parents. This is the child for whom I can still grieve in a very personal and selfish way. This is Annie, who taught me to stay with her agenda first.

There but for the Grace of God: Two Black Women Therapists Explore Privilege

S. Alease Ferguson
Toni C. King

SUMMARY. Within African American society, social class separation has long been a historical factor related to cultural assimilation, within group stratification and distressed relational dynamics. Moving from the macrocosmic to the microcosmic, two African American female therapists share their experience of class privilege dilemmas that surface in their relationships with African American female clients. Typically, privilege intrudes and is felt as either vehement rejection and objectification indicative of class strife, or a shared realization of the need to break free of institutional constraints by choosing to forge connection. Key insights into both the objectifying and growth promoting consequences of this social reality are presented from the vantage point of client and therapist. Three vignettes are presented to illustrate the Black female clients' and therapists' need to speak and feel their truths. Here samples of their dialogue portray-

---

S. Alease Ferguson, PhD, is a therapist. Currently, she holds the position of Grants Manager for the Center for Families and Children in Cleveland, OH. Toni C. King, PhD, is Assistant Professor, Human Development Division of the School of Education and Human Development, State University of New York at Binghamton.

Address correspondence to: Dr. Toni C. King, State University of New York at Binghamton, Division of Human Development, School of Education and Human Development, P.O. Box 6000, Binghamton, NY 13902-6000.

[Haworth co-indexing entry note]: "There but for the Grace of God: Two Black Women Therapists Explore Privilege." Ferguson, S. Alease, and Toni C. King. Co-published simultaneously in *Women & Therapy* (The Haworth Press, Inc.) Vol. 20, No. 1, 1997, pp. 5-14; and: *More than a Mirror: How Clients Influence Therapists' Lives* (ed: Marcia Hill) Harrington Park Press, an imprint of The Haworth Press, Inc., 1997, pp. 5-14. Single or multiple copies of this article are available for a fee from The Haworth Document Delivery Service [1-800-342-9678, 9:00 a.m. - 5:00 p.m. (EST). E-mail address: getinfo@ haworth.com].

ing the dilemmas of class privilege are highlighted as one perplexing element of the therapeutic relationship. *[Article copies available for a fee from The Haworth Document Delivery Service: 1-800-342-9678. E-mail address: getinfo@haworth.com]*

It was a decade ago when we first befriended one another as therapists and doctoral students. As African American females our bond grew out of our own personal life experiences and similar career paths. Our careers were marked by intensive clinical practice in both community based mental health centers and private practice settings. With few if any guideposts about service delivery to African American females, we forged our own mode of social support that involved a process of collegial co-inquiry about our client's lives and our relationships with them. Our ongoing activities to make sense of our clinical interactions have helped us create a template for our own development as African American women and as therapists.

Key among the themes we have discussed is the notion of privilege and how it affects our therapeutic relationships with African American women clients. Time and again, clients have reminded us of the lines of differentiation between "we the therapists" and "they the clients." We share the dilemmas of privilege in therapeutic relationships between therapist and client of the same race and gender to promote understanding of the ways privilege operates to disrupt, block and abort the therapist/client relationship within or across dimensions of difference (e.g., across race, gender, sexuality). We speak about privilege here because we believe Audre Lorde's (1992) wise counsel that unacknowledged class differences rob women of "each other's creative insight."

We define privilege as a place of standing within the social order that allows for a relative sense of power and influence seldom experienced by those with differential positioning. The privileged socioeconomic class among any group are typically those who have attained the hallmarks of educational, economic, career and social success valued by the dominant society. Thus, privileged individuals of varied racial and ethnic groups enjoy a greater likelihood of having their own group characteristics reflected in their immediate world and the larger world around them. Further, these reflections act in ways that support and reinforce self-efficacy, sense of well-being, and goal attainment. Class privilege occurs when this dynamic is driven by class values and norms. It is class privilege that we will discuss as one dynamic that most frequently appears early on within therapeutic encounters with our Black female clients.

Despite the omnipresent nature of privileges and class separation in society, African American women often share a sense of community, kindredness and a ready capacity to engage. Generally, this simpatico between Black women is reflected in the therapeutic setting. We often feel the spark of sisterly appreciation, a sense of immediate recognition from our clients best described as the "I in me" seeing the "I in you." On the other hand, there are also those halting moments where our contacts have been punctuated by sheer and utter rejection . . . a rejection which frequently pivots on the fulcrum of privilege. In such cases verbal projections and fantasies about the black therapist/doctor/woman as a symbol of privilege abound. Our experience is that we are hailed and glamorized on a precarious pedestal. Precarious, because at any moment we may be disparaged. We may see the tenuous doorway we have begun to open with our clients closed right before our eyes. Efforts to bar the channel for further bonding threaten the potential for future work and for growth via this context.

To illustrate the dilemmas of privilege, we present three vignettes. In these vignettes we share comments from women clients which characterize their thoughts and feelings about the class differences between us. Through both individual and group therapeutic sessions, clients impart the meanings of class perceptions they attach to us. Most notably, their interpretations can either open doors to mutual growth and respect or sporadically turn to negative projections that culminate in client shutdown and/or client termination of contact.

Vignette I, Alease's voice:

> The first vignette describes a client's response to my appearance. This incident takes place at a city health center. As a matter of course all of the counselors, doctors and pharmacists dress in casual attire. The guiding premise is that it is critical to break down the barriers of privilege and separation from the client culture. The only time this dress code does not prevail is when it was necessary to advocate for clients at the County Court House, Department of Human Services or at a parole hearing. The first time I met Mrs. P. was the day of a court appearance. In order to prepare for presentation and testimony, I wore a suit and makeup, had manicured hands and freshly styled hair.
>
> I began the session with my normal procedure of introduction, rapport building, noting the services provided and briefly explaining the protocol of therapy. In attempting to assess the client's needs and concerns, I was hit with a barrage of hostile feelings. Mrs. P. began by stating, "Ummh, you must be the boss. No one else here looks like you. I know you got money to go to the beauty shop. Look at

that ring, your man must love you. That suit is expensive, too. There is no way that you can understand me. I've been without a lot of things. People like you can't understand all that. So there is no use in me coming here."

This was my first and most memorable experience of being rebuffed, set apart from another Black woman on the basis of role. The experience was a visceral one, where only physical sensation could precede thought. Hit squarely by four hundred years of rage, I was left rattled, shaken and immobilized. I was so stricken that I could barely speak. My mouth opened but I could not speak. Her biting words and harsh intonation met my temples like angry fists, causing the blood to drain from my head. Somewhat dazed by the emotional attack, I felt myself only able to submit to her decree that we would remain out of each other's lives.

True to her spoken feelings, Mrs. P. never returned. The substance and meaning underlying this abrupt self-termination hit hard. For days, I was keenly affected and saddened by the fact that in this encounter we had been equally objectified, none of our real essence would be shared with the other. Yet I knew that for this client a stasis and separation of our two worlds was needed to preserve safe space and the sustained imagery of differentness.

Here the client perceives the therapist as entrenched in class privilege. The client's acknowledgement of this barrier prevents relationship formation and appreciative inquiry about the client's life, and authentic valuing of where the client is coming from. At worst the therapist is perceived as an imperious and community dissociated woman who has never had any hurtful, deadening and devaluing life experiences. Yet our experience of ourselves as Black women therapists is that we have a "foot in each world. We know how tenuous our grip on one way of life is and how strangling the grip on the other way of life can be" (McClain, 1992, p. 122). As Black women, even the most privileged among us have come to know the ravagement of the soul that societies structured along privileged lines produce and reproduce. We know struggle if not poverty. We know the ongoing battle with race/gender oppression and we have lived alongside destitution. We recognize our families, friends and communities in the women we encounter. Yet sometimes we feel that our task is to bridge the gap and create meaningful contact with clients, despite the seemingly insurmountable intrusion of privilege.

Vignette II, in Alease's voice:

> The second scenario occurs in a support group for crack-cocaine addicted women. One woman commented in an almost quizzical tone: "Dr.___? it must be nice to be a doctor. I bet when you're out in the street nobody ever bothers you because they can tell that you're somebody. You've got a nice car and nice clothes. People can tell that we're nobodies and victims for prey . . . so men try to corrupt us into selling ourselves for some drugs or to feed our kids. Being a doctor protects you. There's no way anyone would try to take you on the street."
>
> Initially, I was impacted by the client's words. An image stirred of me walking through the neighborhood with a sign that said "safe, protected class." Once the image passed I was touched by the candor with which the client spoke. Her truth about our differing circumstances was stunning. I remember wincing at the thought of her words and saying to myself, there is truth in these words. Because I felt no malice in her words, I remained calm and sobered by the realization that this is how we get separated from one another.

In this scenario, it appears that the therapist is being imbued with special powers associated with intellect, social positioning and community status. As the client continued to speak, subvocally I asked myself, are we really that different/disconnected from one another? I also became emotionally flooded by a montage of images reflective of the comfortable and the unsavory elements of my life within the African American community. I remember seeing myself with throngs of black people at weddings, church picnics, funerals, community festivals and political rallies; the streets surrounding my home in a nearby urban black neighborhood; and an act of violence I had witnessed on my way home from school in third grade.

When tuning back into the group energy, I shared my fleeting images and recollections to illustrate both the separation and the commonalities between us. As a group we discussed the truths about the larger and communal societies' view of the "respectable and clean cut" black woman who is afforded certain privileges versus the "goodtime woman" who is vilified and denied respect. Despite the differences of lifestyle, I also highlighted the fact that I, like any woman, was not impervious to violence, rape, mugging or robbery. For me, our commonality as Black women made maltreatment and misplacement of any sister an affront to me and the whole of Black womanhood. Recognizing the potential of the moment we dedicated the next two group sessions to this issue.

Working through this projection was critical in helping the group move forward. During this period all six of the group participants were preparing for community reentry from residential drug treatment. Thus the statement represented a crystallization of critical fears about their own transformations and movement towards the persona of a good and clean living woman. Each had used their nine-month stay in residential treatment to work towards sobriety and to change identities distorted by multiple layers of abuse and degradation. Thus, the ensuing discussion provided an entryway for exploration into the meaning and risks of shedding the non-functional and derogatory identity. As I shared my response to the question and clarification of the projection, the client group began to address their own issues of passage. They surfaced such concerns as: am I doing the necessary work so that those who knew me during my "using times" would see me as now transformed? Would people I encounter view me as clean-cut and respectable? Would the change in my energy field aid me in moving about the community with safety? And though I won't be getting a doctorate anytime soon, what are the steps involved in becoming a more well-put-together Black woman?

A third vignette provides another example:

Vignette III, in Toni's voice:

> This third vignette occurs at a job corps center weekly group counseling session. One young woman client entered the group while still grieving the infant daughter she left at home with her mother in order to attend job corps and attain vocational training. As a new member of the group she resisted any efforts by myself or other participants to facilitate her involvement with brief, abrupt, and often overtly angry responses. During an individual session with me I tried to encourage more discussion about how she felt. She commented vehemently: "You don't's know what I have been through! I'm smart! Don't think you're the only one that can get a college degree. I don't have to be here. I can go to college myself! . . . I don't need this therapy stuff! Why don't you work with the white girls you like so much and leave me alone! My baby and I will be fine! We'll make it without the baby's father and we'll make it without you! So don't be looking down on me!"

Here privilege became the key that opened a doorway to help me understand the client, while simultaneously threatening to close the door to our building a relationship. If the client had not felt our class difference, she would have been less likely to rebuff me in the rawness of her rage.

She let me know the bitterness of her grieving for not only her child, but her abandonment by the baby's father and her loss of her dream to attend college. Foremost, she had experienced the ultimate loss of identity as a self-sufficient person who was not in need of "therapy"!

> Upon hearing the force of the client's feelings, I initially thought/felt "wait a minute! You're way off and your rage is totally misdirected!" At the same time I felt the surge of hope that sometimes accompanies a client's emotional release. I had already known that she was angry. In her outburst, however, she had provided me with answers as to why she was angry and withdrawn. Still I wondered if this moment was a breakthrough to improved relations between us or simply a breakdown. Would she choose to take another step in the process of therapy with me? Or, would she close the door and move emotionally beyond reach?
>
> Prior to the client's outburst, I knew that much of this client's anger during group counseling was levied directly at me. From this anger, I felt her projection of me placed me in the role of the "judgmental mother," the mythic mother image or authority person in her life who believed she would fail. The force of her feelings let me know that she felt tremendous threat to her identities as woman, mother, student and her sense of agency and self-determination. I experienced her as a group member for whom everything I said or did was perceived as an act of violation to reinforce the feelings that she did not measure up to a standard integral to her self-valuing. I felt as if she'd drawn a boundary I could not cross. I was intimidated by her silent fury and angered by what I perceived to be her disavowal (and disallowal) of my goodwill. My persona as therapist, that for many of the corps women was coherent and authentic, appeared to be experienced by this client as fragmented and annihilative. I felt frustrated and helpless to convey my motives and good intent.
>
> After the client expressed her anger in our individual session, I felt the familiar tug of memories and emotions linked to previous intrusions of class separation in my early life. These memories seemed to arise in response to my silent internal query of when did "it" all begin? When did my "class" privileges accrue to the point of making this painful moment of separation inevitable? I recalled getting beaten up repeatedly by Black kids from "cross the tracks" because I attended parochial elementary school. I vividly remembered feeling that I was "seen differently" by many of the Black kids in the newly integrated junior high school after submitting a short story to the school newspaper writing contest. I also remem-

bered the pennies my Grandfather helped me save for college from the age of six, and the used set of encyclopedias my mother purchased to help my sister and I with our homework when I was eight. These memory glyphs swept past me, locating me in a raced and gendered, socioeconomic space.

My initial response was to sit in the moment, breathe deeply and to let these impressions move through me. I looked hard at the client to convey attention, respect and honor for the hard hurting that she was bearing up under. After a few long moments, I responded to her tirade by describing the current tension as I saw it–that she was ambitious as I was, but had not had as much help. I said as much. I did not need to dismantle her rage, or attempt to step into her grieving space at the time. I felt that the relentlessly cruel reality of our differences in class positioning threatened to rob us of potential connection. Hence in that moment, I chose to work only with what I felt was least painful, less raw, and also more tangible: her desire to achieve and to attend college.

Over the next weeks she continued to reject me, but her rejection carried increasingly less bitterness. I had her interest. I sensed that she respected my not overstepping her boundaries. At the end of the six-month term, she made a decision to return home to her child. She later wrote to tell me that she was working as a taxi driver, had reconciled with the child's father, had plans to marry him and that she still wanted to go to college.

What is poignant about all of these stories is that many of these clients have an initial spark of interest and desire to bond with us as positive models of womanhood and sisterhood. Their eyes light up and they look admiringly at us, often openly appreciating our outward persona (e.g., attire, hair, professionalism, confidence) as well as our achievement. Yet this admiration can become the proverbial "salt in the wound" when clients feel that their lives compare unfavorably to ours. As therapists we are engaged in a struggle to help our clients relate to their own life stories in more loving ways. We walk a thin line when this client admiration turns to understandable rage, envy, resentment or more general feelings of self-deprecation, despair and hopelessness.

All too often we and our clients, both, realize that commonalities of race and gender experience are buffeted by social class. Yet, they sometimes see their life stories in relationship to their fantasies about our lives. These fantasies include notions that we come from "perfectly functional family units" that approach The Cosby Show in amicable family relationships as well as affluence and ease. Other clients sometimes feel that we may have worked hard, and that we were strengthened by the perfect conditions of educational preparation, socialization, family support and financial security.

Even more damaging is the notion that when we did encounter struggle, temptation, hardships or choice points (due to prior socialization in "happy" families), we were perfectly programmed to make all the right choices. This particular projection tells us that the client is engaging in destructive self-blaming processes. She is casting herself in the role of one who has been duped, gullible, "taken" – one who has made all the wrong choices and now has a long road ahead just to "break even." At such times, the mildest interventions and even expressions of support can be hurtled back at us with a well-tooled venom and rage that only one's "sister" could devise. Sonia Sanchez (1989) speaks of this deep knowledge of another being used in anger as a "wounding in the house of a friend."

As therapists we are often baffled and hurt by such wounding, packaged in accusations and allegations that skillfully move under the skin. The client's rage claws at our fragile foothold in white society, finding our weaknesses and collusive posturing within organizations defined along white hegemonic values. We often see these accusations in our clients' eyes before these admonishments reach their lips. We sense the accusation, even before our clients "come to voice" their objections and rejections of us–and hence of themselves, for not being one of "us." Before they consciously compare, fall short and then blame us, we see the point of tension. We viscerally feel the battle lines being drawn and we mentally prepare ourselves for the lessons of privilege we will learn. At times the issue is clearly their's, the clients', and we merely stand in what Martin Buber (1970) refers to as the clarity of our being. Our process becomes one of holding a loving image of the client as whole, a survivor, able to work through yet another element that would reduce her full humanness. At other times we are sucked into the many vortexes of woman-to-woman issues before we are clear enough to honor the richness of our differences in ways that permit entry and foster working through, rather than exclusion and write-off.

Facing down these issues of privilege with our clients is important to us. We link this significance to the pain which class privileges have created within group for Black-on-Black relationships and communities both historically and currently. When we succeed we feel connected to core values handed down to us in the form of a Biblical proverb. From our mothers and their mothers before them echoes the chant, "there but for the grace of God, go I." Each of us (and we believe, countless other Black women) has internalized a value central to the ethos of African American culture that a power greater than ourselves is the determining factor in our particular privileges. Although we must make the most of any favorable conditions in our lives, we must simultaneously recognize that if the conditions of our upbringing (both moral and economic) had been different, we could be experiencing the struggles of our clients.

REFERENCES

Buber, M. (1970). *I and thou*. NY: Scribner.

hooks, b. (1994). *Sisters of the yam*. Boston, MA: Southside.

Lorde, A. (1992). Age, race, class, and sex: Women redefining difference. In M.L. Anderson, & P.H. Collins (Eds.), *Race, class, and gender: An anthology* (pp. 495-503). Belmont, CA: Wadsworth Publishing Company.

McClain, L. (1992). The middle class black's burden. In M.L. Anderson, & P. H. Collins (Eds.), *Race, class, and gender: An anthology*. (pp. 120-122). Belmont, CA: Wadsworth Publishing Company.

Sanchez, S. (1989). Lecture Notes. Presentation, Norfolk State University.

Hope

Michele Clark

SUMMARY. The author describes her treatment of her first alcoholic client and observes how the process of providing hope to this client heightened the author's personal capacity to hope. Hope as an aspect of healing is considered and personal reflections on psychotherapeutic work with alcoholics are discussed. *[Article copies available for a fee from The Haworth Document Delivery Service: 1-800-342-9678. E-mail address: getinfo@haworth.com]*

The workshop has ended and people are gathering leaflets and disposing of paper coffee cups. A woman comes up to me, the leader; she presses my hand and says, "I'm so glad you're out there doing this kind of work." The implication is that working with alcoholics is so depressing that she's glad there's someone who wants to take it on. Yet the theme of my workshop was that *alcoholism is a hopeful problem*. Nevertheless, I know that she has the same stereotypes I did before I began this work. In particular, before my first alcoholic client, a woman in her mid-twenties, definitively changed the direction of my work as a psychotherapist.

There was no alcoholism in my immediate or extended family; there was no abuse, no poverty, no instability. Yet I spent much of my childhood, teens and twenties doing battle with unrelenting self-critical and

Michele Clark, LICMHC, CAC, works at Champlain Drug and Alcohol Services and teaches psychology in the Adult Degree Program of Vermont College.

Address correspondence to: Michele Clark, RR 1, Box 2262, Plainfield, VT 05667.

[Haworth co-indexing entry note]: "Hope." Clark, Michele. Co-published simultaneously in *Women & Therapy* (The Haworth Press, Inc.) Vol. 20, No. 1, 1997, pp. 15-21; and: *More than a Mirror: How Clients Influence Therapists' Lives* (ed: Marcia Hill) Harrington Park Press, an imprint of The Haworth Press, Inc., 1997, pp. 15-21. Single or multiple copies of this article are available for a fee from The Haworth Document Delivery Service [1-800-342-9678, 9:00 a.m. - 5:00 p.m. (EST). E-mail address: getinfo@ haworth.com].

fearful thoughts; one set would be vanquished and soon another would emerge, noisy as the first, clamoring for attention. Like many American-Jewish families, mine functioned with a continually high level of anxiety (Friedman, 1982). This cultural trait made itself known to me in dark natterings. As a child these thoughts made me anxious, quick to tears and easily hurt, as a teen they made me defiant and wild, in my twenties they made me depressed.

In my teens and twenties, I placated the dark thoughts with hours of talk with my women friends about their problems and my own. In talking I found my way into several of the elements which Irwin Yalom (1985) lists as necessary for change and growth: catharis, I spoke the bad feelings and so felt less trapped in them; universality, my friends told me their troubles and I felt that I was not alone; altruism, my friends thought I was a good listener, it was helpful to talk to me. Together these produced some of that energy-giving medium—hope—which is a "crucial . . . required" (Yalom, 1985, p. 6) part of any personal change process. For me, at least, hope is a physical as well as a mental event. When I feel that surge of it, up from the diaphragm, pressing against my heart, I am able to act, go forward, or try something new.

After I received my Master's degree I joined the Women's Mental Health Collective, a small non-profit clinic, where the collegial norm was an easy openness about personal insecurities. And so, in both my work with clients and my collegial life I was imbedded in conversations about psychological struggles. In the doing of psychotherapy and in theoretical and personal talks with my colleagues, I experienced daily doses of catharsis, universality, altruism and hope. Not that I understood all of this at the time, it is only in looking back.

The family therapist Michael Elkin has suggested, somewhat ironically, that "Therapists are the only people . . . who need 25 hours of therapy per week" (Treadway, 1991). This was certainly true for me at that time. Another way to put it is that I had a chronic hope deficit and the practice of therapy, first, eased my shame at having such a deficit, and second, helped me fill it.

But, of course, as a therapist, one has many failures. Clients don't all improve; the process is long and slow and just when you think someone has turned a corner, her old issues return. So I didn't get hope every day—not as much as I wanted and needed. It was within this context of my continual need for infusions of hope that my first work with an alcoholic woman occurred.

* * *

Alcoholism hadn't been mentioned in the Masters degree program which I completed in 1974. Although, in my first work environment of the Women's Mental Health Collective there was a representative of every mental health discipline, none of the staff had had more than a cursory training in chemical dependence. We held the same stereotypes that everyone else in the society held: an alcoholic is a flagrantly drunk working-class man.

In 1976 the Women's Alcoholism Program of Cambridge, Massachusetts offered us six sessions of training about women and alcohol (Finkelstein, Duncan, Derman, & Smeltz, 1990). The training involved, among other things, meetings with mature sober alcoholic women who spoke with us about their alcohol dependence and the recovery process. We accompanied the trainers to AA and Alanon meetings. The sober alcoholic women who came to speak with us and the men and women we witnessed speaking at the AA and Alanon meetings seemed wise, responsible, integrated, compassionate and brave. While the Women's Program introduced us to the 12-Step programs, their services were geared to women who were the "invisible alcoholics" and often could not make use of AA because of its male oriented norms (Sandmaier, 1981).

We were immediately enthusiastic about these resources. We had all developed our values in the left wing of the anti-war movement and we felt that in AA, Alanon and the Women's Alcoholism Program, we had found examples of grassroots mental health work which fit into our ideal model of a society without experts.

In response, the first thing we changed in our clinic protocols was our intake procedure. To our usual questions we added: *Do you ever worry about your own use of alcohol?* Our second new guideline was that if a woman answered yes to this question, we would explore her answer in the first session and then try, as soon as possible, to refer her either to AA or to the Women's Alcoholism Program since group was the treatment of choice for this primary problem. The trainers had warned us about *enabling* which meant, among other things, trying to help a woman with other life problems while she continued to abuse alcohol. This, they assured us, would lead nowhere, and would confirm for the client the idea that if only her other problems improved, her drinking would not be a problem. Their diagnostic message was strong: alcoholism is the primary problem and has to be addressed first and directly.

In practice, this message proved difficult to implement. Women who were in trouble with alcohol were not able to accept this insight in one or two sessions. So it seemed that, what we actually would do was refer a client to the Women's Alcoholism Program and she would not return to see one of us, nor follow our referral.

Such was my experience when I encountered the first alcoholic client with whom I was successful. I first met with Donna on a Friday afternoon at the end of summer. No one else was in the office and the city had that shut-down feeling of summer weekends. Donna was in her mid-twenties, she wore jeans and a baggy flannel shirt. She took a seat in one of the swivel chairs, turning her profile to me. Since her profile was mainly covered by her long, straight hair, I spent most of the first session, and in fact, most of our subsequent sessions, talking to a part of her nose and chin.

I was nervous about asking about her drinking because, even though she had mentioned it in the intake, my experience up to that time was that when I asked a woman about her use of alcohol she became defensive and angry. Then I would get that sinking feeling that I didn't know what to do next. However, Donna began to talk about her alcohol use as soon as I asked about it. She told me she often had blackouts, she had once been charged with DWI; she had almost killed herself in a car accident which she couldn't remember happening. "The only thing I remember is getting into the car after the party, and then looking at the dashboard of the car pushed up against the stop sign."

When I suggested, gently I hoped, the Women's Alcoholism Program, she told me, angrily, no way. And, anyway, she said, "I didn't come here because of my drinking." She had really come to talk about her problems at work, she worked too many hours at a shelter for teenagers and she didn't know how to tell the boss she needed to cut back. In her DWI program she had been forced to go to AA meetings which she described to me as "these disgusting old guys talking about getting laid and not re-membering it." I mentioned that the Women's Program had been set up to address women's needs, particularly. But she wasn't having any of it.

So, I thought to myself, here's someone with a life threatening drinking problem, who won't go to either AA or the Women's Program, what am I supposed to do now? If I insist she go, I'm doing the right thing, but she won't go. If I allow her to continue to work with me, am I *enabling*?

We spent the rest of the session talking about her life in general, her work, her roommates. She said that she felt comfortable with me, and would like to return next week. Knowing that I should plan to refer her out either now or in our next session, and knowing that if I did, she wouldn't go, I quickly made two decisions. First, I wouldn't refer her out, and second, I wouldn't present her in our weekly case review of new clients, thereby assuring that no one could criticize me or accuse me of enabling. I left the session with a buoyant, almost elated feeling, not knowing why. I thought the elation resulted from my sense of being a defiant bad girl who had the delicious task of keeping a secret.

I continued to meet with Donna and in each session she discussed her use of alcohol in greater depth. Each session I was surprised, although reassured by this. She was not in denial; she knew she was in a lot of trouble with alcohol. But she had never known anyone who had been able to stop drinking. Her father was alcoholic and so were both her brothers. She may never have known another woman who was alcoholic. In each session she would ask me, directly, "Do you think there's any hope for me?" And in each session I would tell her stories of what I had seen at AA, and in the Women's Program, how much hope I had witnessed, and how impressed I had been. I told her the same stories over again because these were the only ones I knew. Although the stories weren't about me, personally, as I told them to Donna I put myself at the scene of my training and described what I had experienced with the feeling and enthusiasm I had felt when I heard them. Sometimes we would have this hope-seeking, hope-giving dialogue more than once in a session.

I continued to leave our session with the buoyant, light feeling which I attributed to the secrecy factor. Finally, after six sessions I felt confident that I was doing the right thing and I presented Donna in case review. The response was supportive. My colleagues thought all was going well because, as I could see, in each session we explored the impact and nature of her drinking. There was no imperative about sending her to the Women's Program, as long as drinking continued to be a primary focus of our work.

Because I thought the secrecy was the cause of that post-session buoyance, I assumed that once I included Donna in case review, the feeling would pass. But no, there it was, after Donna and I finished our session, on Friday afternoon, as I walked to my car, as I drove to my house, there it still was. This feeling continued to be a gift to me after each of our sessions for the next four months that I worked with her. Even though our work together went into the early winter, I remember those Friday afternoons as always sunny and warm, filled with hope.

Donna stopped drinking for a week or two, started again, stopped. Finally she did accept a referral to the Women's Alcoholism Program. I accompanied her to her initial appointment with them. She eventually joined a group there and developed a strong sobriety.

*   *   *

In my individual psychotherapy work with Donna, where I was, ostensibly, only the giver of hope, I was, as much as my client, a receiver of hope. I received something similar to what I believe alcoholics receive when they go to AA meetings. For at these moments, the counseling process became similar to the process which occurs in AA where giving and receiving merge. My capacity to feel optimistic and, therefore, to calm myself, rose significantly, at least for the rest of the day. If there were a way to physiologically measure hope–lower pulse rate or blood pressure? higher serotonin levels?–mine, like members of AA at the end of a meeting, had surely changed toward the optimal.

In the months that followed I began to choose actively new clients who indicated drinking was a problem. I developed ever more interesting ways of talking with a woman about her drinking without raising her defenses, because now I knew I could do it in an individual mode as a kind of therapeutic foyer to a group resource. I felt, though it wasn't true, that in this individual mode, I was inventing something entirely new. Gradually, I became the specialist on chemical dependence at the Collective. I went from strength to strength; I had several "successes" in a row. "Success" was defined as the client becoming sober and joining some kind of support group to deepen her capacity to abstain from alcohol.

Six years ago I moved to another state and now my psychotherapy work is, almost exclusively, with alcoholics, or in human services training around issues of chemical dependence. In my local community I am the person to call to give a talk or a training about women and alcohol. I would like to say that I still get buoyant after every session, the way I did with Donna, but I don't. I still like the work and find it hopeful. It is also true that I don't need infusions of hope the way I did in the past. Perhaps I need hope less because so many alcoholic clients have allowed me to gain so much extra hope; perhaps it is because of my own continuing maturation. Probably it is a combination of both. And, sometimes, still, there are those moments. For example, the other night a friend of mine told me a story about her father who had just died at the age of seventy-eight. "Two years ago," she said, "he joined AA, and a few weeks ago he told my mother that these past two years were the best two years of his life. My mother thought that was really true. At the funeral, people came up to me and said how he'd changed, how he was really starting to show compassion, not just judging and criticizing." And I feel again that warm surge of optimism and gratitude, that, even towards the end of life, personal transformation is possible.

REFERENCES

Finkelstein, N., Duncan, S., Derman, L., & Smeltz, J. (1990). Getting sober, getting well. Cambridge, MA: Women's Alcoholism Program.

Friedman, E. (1982). The myth of the shiksa. *Ethnicity and family therapy* (pp. 429-526). New York: Guilford.

Sandmaier, Marian (1981). *The invisible alcoholics*. New York: McGraw-Hill.

Treadway, D. (1991, January/February). Codependency: disease, metaphor, or fad? *The Family Networker*, pp. 39-42.

Yalom, I. (1985). *The theory and practice of group psychotherapy*. New York: Basic Books.

Bearing Witness to the Unspeakable

Marta Y. Young

SUMMARY. This article examines the experience of a therapist in a therapeutic relationship with a woman who had survived physical and sexual torture. In particular, the short and long-term impact of this client's ordeal on the therapist as a clinician, clinical trainer and researcher is described. *[Article copies available for a fee from The Haworth Document Delivery Service: 1-800-342-9678. E-mail address: getinfo@haworth.com]*

When I first found out about this collection, I was immediately flooded with memories of clients who had challenged me and deeply touched me. I remembered my intense feelings of grief while attending a moving memorial service for a longstanding client who had died of AIDS, my frustration dealing with an extremely depressed teenager and my joy at seeing a survivor of childhood sexual abuse put together the pieces of her life puzzle. There is one client, however, whose courage and determination to survive have had a powerful and profound impact on me as a person and as a clinician.

During the third year of my doctoral program in clinical psychology, I started feeling stifled by small town Ontario and by the walls of academe. Furthermore, my dissertation on the adjustment of Salvadoran refugees

Marta Y. Young, PhD, is a feminist psychologist and cross-cultural researcher who is interested in the adaptation of immigrant and refugee women. She is currently Assistant Professor in clinical psychology at the University of Ottawa.

Address correspondence to: Marta Y. Young, Centre for Psychological Services, University of Ottawa, 11 Marie Curie Drive, Ottawa, Ontario, K1N 6N5, Canada.

[Haworth co-indexing entry note]: "Bearing Witness to the Unspeakable." Young, Marta Y. Co-published simultaneously in *Women & Therapy* (The Haworth Press, Inc.) Vol. 20, No. 1, 1997, pp. 23-25; and: *More than a Mirror: How Clients Influence Therapists' Lives* (ed: Marcia Hill) Harrington Park Press, an imprint of The Haworth Press, Inc., 1997, pp. 23-25. Single or multiple copies of this article are available for a fee from The Haworth Document Delivery Service [1-800-342-9678, 9:00 a.m. - 5:00 p.m. (EST). E-mail address: getinfo@haworth.com].

23

had sharpened my sensitivity to refugee issues and had reawakened my need to be in contact with people from other cultures. I joined a local Central American solidarity committee and I also started volunteering as a therapist at the local resettlement agency in London, Ontario.

One of the first clients referred to me was a middle-aged Chilean woman who had been a professor of philosophy in Santiago. The sessions were conducted in Spanish as I had lived during my childhood in several Central and South American countries. During the initial session, Juana proceeded to relate to me her experiences in Chile after the assassination of Allende in 1973. She had been incarcerated on six occasions between 1973 and 1988 before fleeing with her family to Canada. The pattern of arrests was similar: each time there was a loud thumping at the door in the middle of the night and she would be dragged into a black unidentified car by four military personnel and detained for several weeks at a time. After describing the arrests, Juana fell silent as though unsure how to broach the next part of her story. I gently asked her if she felt comfortable sharing with me her experiences in detention. Juana immediately launched into a very rapid and intense recounting of this period of her life. For over an hour, she provided detailed accounts of the severe physical and sexual torture she had experienced. With great shame and emotion, she also described how she had been forced to torture and to engage in sexual activity with fellow prisoners, several of whom were cherished colleagues and friends.

Throughout this session, I found myself struggling to remain present as an empathetic therapist as Juana related the horrific ordeal she had undergone. It was not until the session was over, however, that I became fully aware of the impact Juana's story had had on me. I remember walking home in an almost dazed fashion, barely greeting my partner and zeroing in on the futon couch in the living room of my apartment. I remember distinctly turning the lights off and lying in the dark for what seemed an indefinite period of time. My initial response was to burst into tears and feel very angry at the perpetrators. I also felt despair at the violence in the world and intense empathy for the pain Juana had had to endure. I was then flooded with many of the torture scenes Juana had described to me. At times, this reexperiencing was so vivid that I felt compelled to discuss them with my partner who was understandably reluctant to hear the painful details. During the course of the week, I continued to have intrusive recollections that gradually dissipated over the following months.

In addition to the more immediate response described above, this session has also had a longer range impact on me as an individual, therapist and clinical supervisor. From a personal standpoint, I found that bearing witness to Juana's pain has sensitized me in a much deeper way than books or solidarity meetings to the horrors of war, persecution and torture. It has strengthened my commitment and my resolve to work in the area of traumatology as a clinician, researcher, and advocate. Juana also taught me, at an early stage in my clinical career, that human beings are incredibly resilient and that despite despairing moments there is hope. As a clinician, I learned the importance of caring for myself and the wisdom in recognizing my emotional limits. I try to ensure, for example, that my caseload does not include a disproportionate number of survivors of trauma. I also regularly meet with feminist colleagues for peer supervision and I attend a support group of women psychologists. Furthermore, in my role as clinical trainer and supervisor, I find myself being particularly attentive to my students' reactions to clients, particularly those who are survivors of domestic violence, childhood sexual abuse or torture.

Recently, I received news that Juana had successfully retrained and that her family was adjusting well to life in Canada. I feel greatly privileged that Juana has shared with me her pain and her suffering as well as her hope for the future. As Sandra Butler (1995) stated so eloquently, "I have come to understand that each moment shimmers with the possibility of tikkun olam, which is to live in the knowledge that each moment contains within it the possibility of mending, repairing and transforming the world" (p. 112).

REFERENCE

Butler, S. (1995). The fitting room. *Women & Therapy, 17,* 103-112.

Joining the Expedition:
Journal of a Therapist-in-Training

Susan E. Lillich

SUMMARY. Although there is a plethora of practical, skill-based guidance available to student therapists, the internal aspects of young therapists' training period are often neglected. This journal explores the experiences of one psychology graduate student as she traverses a year of clinical training. *[Article copies available for a fee from The Haworth Document Delivery Service: 1-800-342-9678. E-mail address: getinfo@haworth.com]*

A psychology professor once told me that people have two basic fantasies about their therapy: that it will end, and that it will never end (Kessler, personal communication). Many graduate student therapists have the same fantasies about their formal training period. Sometimes our work goes smoothly, and interactions with clients, colleagues, and supervisors nourish our development. On those days, we bask in the glow of a supportive, intellectually rich and diverse training atmosphere and wonder what we will do without it when our graduate school days are over. Other days, when the needs of a client in crisis consume time allocated for writing the

---

Susan Lillich is a doctoral student in clincal psychology at the University of Vermont.

The author acknowledges with gratitude the guidance and support of Drs. Christine Wells and Karen Fondacaro.

Address correspondence to: Susan Lillich, Department of Psychology, John Dewey Hall, University of Vermont, Burlington, VT 05405.

[Haworth co-indexing entry note]: "Joining the Expedition: Journal of a Therapist-in-Training." Lillich, Susan E. Co-published simultaneously in *Women & Therapy* (The Haworth Press, Inc.) Vol. 20, No. 1, 1997, pp. 27-33; and: *More than a Mirror: How Clients Influence Therapists' Lives* (ed: Marcia Hill) Harrington Park Press, an imprint of The Haworth Press, Inc., 1997, pp. 27-33. Single or multiple copies of this article are available for a fee from The Haworth Document Delivery Service [1-800-342-9678, 9:00 a.m. - 5:00 p.m. (EST). E-mail address: getinfo@haworth.com].

dissertation or a supervisor requests that we write yet another report by the end of the week, the training period seems endless and we dream of the day when we will be degreed and, we fantasize, "free." Volumes have been published on the subject of learning psychotherapy–the hows, whens, wheres, and whys of being a professional therapist. Yet there are few narrative accounts of young therapists' early experiences on the expedition: what maps guide us, and how do we learn to read them? Do we put stock in the measurements of the external compasses, or let our internal compass be our guide? When the arrows on the two compasses point in different directions, which one do we heed? The following are selected notes from a pre-doctoral internship year: the first time I ventured to join the expedition.

JULY

I arrive at the clinic and place my belongings in the intern's office, mine for the next twelve months. It is the second year of my doctoral training in psychology, and to this point my experience as a therapist consists of six months in the college counseling center, carrying two or three clients at a time. As soon as I enter the clinic, I know my experience here will be different. Two phones are ringing; a woman jiggling a crying infant stands at the reception desk; the waiting room is filled to overflowing with children, from toddlers to teenagers, and an array of parents, social workers, and other caretakers. For the next year, I am to work here twenty hours per week, doing therapy with the children and families the clinic serves. On my off days, I will attend classes and pursue my research projects.

A few days later, I meet my first clients, an 11-year-old girl and her parents. They are requesting family therapy after several months of individual therapy have failed to produce the effect for which they had hoped: the cessation of their frequent, often violent family arguments. I invite them into my office; they settle themselves and look anxiously at one another and, expectantly, at me. Already, I am painfully aware that I share their assumption that I am in charge here: my agency, my office, my lead. Indeed, as the session begins I do nothing to challenge this shared belief. I ask questions, they answer; I nod, they continue; I paraphrase, they concur. In this hour, I am suddenly thrust into the role of teacher when I have so long been student; the role of expert when everywhere else I am known to be a novice. The dissonance created by these competing assumptions is startling, so much so that I become quiet. I am sure my clients notice my silence, and I wonder what they are thinking as they continue to speak, sharing what they want me to know. Near the end of the hour, I suggest weekly family therapy sessions. I tell them that I am an intern and will be working at the agency for one year. I notice that, for the first time, all three family members agree on something: that they will not still need to be in therapy a year from now. The mere thought of such a prospect brings smiles to their faces. They are quite certain that their conflicts will be resolved long before next July. I am less hopeful than they, but I so much want to agree with them: yes, if you come to therapy things will get better before too long. As much as they, I do not want to acknowledge fully the long, arduous, confusing path which lies ahead. It is impossible for any of us to anticipate where we will stumble and fall and where we will traverse the rocks with confidence. We agree simply to meet next week, and to begin.

AUGUST

I take a long-planned trip to the Pacific Northwest, with the dual purpose of visiting my friend and mentor, Kate, and spending some time in the wilderness, grieving. It is six months since my mother, age 54, died unexpectedly. A few days into my trip, my father phones to tell me that my grandmother, a near and dear presence in my life, is barely clinging to her own. She is not expected to survive the day, and my father suggests that I prepare to fly east for her funeral. Though Grandma had recently been unwell, there were no indications of an impending rapid decline in her health, and I am surprised by my father's call. Feeling cheated out of my vacation and overwhelmed by the loss of a woman my sister and I have dubbed our "third parent," I leave Kate's loving cocoon and travel to New York. The now-familiar rituals of the funeral and mourning period go smoothly, and I miss only one additional day of work at the clinic. Though my colleagues and friends are supportive and inquire about me and my family, I do not speak much of this death. I grieve quietly, both for my mother and grandmother and for my radically altered sense of family. I find it difficult to work with my child and adolescent clients who have conflicts with their mothers, and with mothers who do not seem to understand the importance of their presence in their children's lives. Since the majority of my caseload is comprised of families struggling with these issues, my difficulties are problematic, and they become my first true lessons in dealing with what my professors have been calling "countertransference." When a mother and her fifteen-year-old daughter leave my office after spending most of their session arguing bitterly, I weep. I feel powerless to help them alter the patterns in which they are entrenched, and angry with them for marring their togetherness with such hatred and conflict. I yearn still to have a mother, even one with whom to fight. I speak of these feelings, and my concerns about them, with my supervisor and my peers. They are empathic and offer helpful suggestions and guidelines, but they have mothers. I do not feel truly understood, and I wonder whether any of my clients feels understood by me.

OCTOBER

Since July, I have been seeing five siblings who are currently living in foster care, as a condition of their return to their mother's custody. The eldest, who is nine, begins to exhibit sexualized play with dolls and with her younger siblings. Additionally, she is falling behind in school, and since extended visits with her biological mother began, she often refuses to speak. In my office, she hides under the desk or table, making animal sounds. In their sessions, her younger siblings startle when a person walks by in the hallway or a truck passes outside. I have serious concerns about all the children, but their discharge from foster care is a fait accompli, and it occurs on schedule. Six weeks after regaining custody, their mother ceases bringing the children to therapy, and I am unable to convince her even of the need for a termination session.

In wondering what will become of these children, I hope for the best, but fear the worst. Other professionals involved with the family seem unconcerned that the children have been pulled from therapy. I find comfort by telling myself that school personnel and social workers will surely notice the children's difficulties sooner or later, but even after only three months in this job, I am learning that this is not necessarily so. I wonder what I could have done to help this mother feel more comfortable with therapy and with me. At this stage of my training, whenever something goes wrong in a treatment, I always first ask what mistakes I have made. It is an appropriate first question, but a difficult one to ask . . . and even more difficult to answer.

JANUARY

Sitting in on a psychiatric consultation with one of my child clients, I watch and listen as his mother becomes more and more distraught. She speaks of feeling alone and misunderstood. She feels as if no one knows what a difficult life she has had, and no one is willing to help her so that her son will not face the same difficulties. She mentions how sad she and her child have felt at the recent death of her mother, who was a constant presence in the lives of both of them. The psychiatrist and I share that we, too, lost our mothers this year. Our self-disclosure is met with tears and anger. Though she is sure that we miss our mothers, she feels that we cannot truly understand her, for she has had much misfortune in her life. She is unlike us, for she does not have a good job, nice clothes, expensive cars, and happy families, and she is certain that we do. When the psychiatrist declines to prescribe medication for her son, she storms out of the clinic, enraged. She phones me later, still defensive, but reaching out. She wishes to schedule next week's session. I am drained, both physically and emotionally, as I imagine she is also . . . two women in very different places, both mourning.

In the days and months to come I will think about this encounter many times. I had felt that my friends and colleagues didn't understand my grief because their mothers hadn't died, yet my client feels misunderstood when I disclose my similarity to her. Just as clients sometimes believe (mistakenly or not) that a therapist with whom they share a certain characteristic will be more empathic, therapists sometimes believe that their disclosure of similarity to the client will be accepted with relief and gratitude. In this case, what my client felt to be an insignificant interface of our experience paled in comparison to the many large ways in which she perceived our lives to differ. While I could not necessarily have predicted my client's response when I shared my personal experience, this encounter taught me to consider carefully the possible impact on the client of any self-disclosure. I learned that it is easy to make a disclosure in the name of "empathy" when I am (consciously or not) feeling anxious or overwhelmed by the client's material, and that both similarities and differences between client and therapist are powerful factors in the therapy relationship.

APRIL

It is the beginning of her session, and my eight-year-old client and I are drawing pictures together. As we work, she asks me several questions. "Did your daddy ever hit your mommy?" she wants to know. "Did your daddy ever hit you?" she asks. Her daddy did those things. Her daddy also repeatedly sexually abused her, and she is starting to understand that this is something which daddies aren't supposed to do. I listen and respond as she talks about these experiences, and wonder silently whether I am asking the right questions and saying the right things. She has never told anyone about these experiences. Though I have worked with several children who have been sexually and/or physically abused, this is the first time that I have been the first person to whom a child has come with her confusion and pain. I tell her that she is correct and brave to tell me. She says her daddy swore that he would kill her mommy if she told anyone. We talk with her mother, who is sensitive and supportive. Later that day, when I call in a report to the state abuse hotline, I am interviewed by an investigator who asks for information which I do not have. He accepts the report, but is clearly displeased by my inability to provide more detailed answers to his many questions. Again, the familiar doubts: have I done my job competently? In my attempt to be clinically sensitive, did I neglect to gather information needed to facilitate the investigation of this abusive man who has hurt his child so profoundly? I have received no training on how to handle disclosures of abuse or how to decide what must be reported, yet in the past nine months I have had several children and parents describe situations which, under state law, constitute abuse or neglect. I am fortunate to have an experienced supervisor with whom to consult, but I dislike this feeling of being part therapist, part police officer. Often this year, I have wished for some benevolent, omniscient presence to oversee my work with these children and make wise decisions about what is best for them . . . but none has appeared.

JUNE

Though I have told all my clients that I am in training, it comes as a surprise to many when I remind them that I will soon be leaving the agency. Of all the families with whom I work, I most dread telling the couple and their eleven-year-old with whom I shared that first anxious session nearly one year ago. They have come to therapy once, sometimes twice weekly since then, not missing an appointment all year. Their therapy has been exceedingly difficult for all of us, but their commitment to it is unsurpassed by any client I have ever seen, and we have forged a strong bond. I do not want to leave them, and their reactions to the news of my impending departure–anger, sadness, and helplessness–are so close to my own feelings about the deaths of my mother and grandmother that they linger throughout the last weeks of my internship.

The goodbyes occur, and my work here is finished. My new internship, on the pediatric floor of my university's hospital, begins in less than a week. My dissertation looms large, piles of data staring at me each time I sit down at the computer. It has been a challenging year, both professionally and personally, and one in which I have taken baby steps–sometimes backward, but mostly, I hope, forward along the path upon which I have unquestionably now embarked. It has been an expedition through unfamiliar territory. Clinically, I have had the good fortune to work, under the supervision of a competent, good-humored supervisor, with many children and families; I have learned the importance of trying to meet them where they are, though that has often meant heading into territory which I cannot locate on my map. Personally, I have begun to adjust to my shifting identity. I think of myself less often now primarily as someone's daughter or granddaughter, and this alteration has created space for further development of other aspects of my self. I have learned that in order to be helpful to others, I must also meet myself where I am, in grief or confusion or joy. I am a young woman, a sister, a lover, a friend, and a therapist. I have joined the expedition, and I am honored to be part of it.

Lessons Learned:
A Psychologist's Perspective
on Psychotherapy

Wendy S. Pachter

SUMMARY. Psychotherapy exerts effects on both therapist and client. This article describes personal and professional lessons learned by a clinical psychologist in the course of outpatient therapy and consultation at a community health center. The effects of listening to stories of major trauma, the resilience of human spirit and relationships, the role of the therapist's feelings in psychotherapy, and the power of therapeutic interventions are discussed. *[Article copies available for a fee from The Haworth Document Delivery Service: 1-800-342-9678. E-mail address: getinfo@haworth.com]*

During and immediately following my graduate training in clinical psychology, I practiced as a psychologist at a rural community health center. I saw individuals of all ages, as well as couples and families. I saw wealthy, highly educated people as well as people with little by way of financial or educational resources. I had previously worked with heroin

Wendy S. Pachter received her PhD in clinical psychology from The University of Vermont in 1984 and her JD from Columbia University School of Law in 1988. She is currently a mediator and consultant on professional-client relationships, ethics and public policy issues.

Address correspondence to: Wendy S. Pachter, 3721 39th Street, N.W., #A-193, Washington, DC 20016-5520.

[Haworth co-indexing entry note]: "Lessons Learned: A Psychologist's Perspective on Psychotherapy." Pachter, Wendy S. Co-published simultaneously in *Women & Therapy* (The Haworth Press, Inc.) Vol. 20, No. 1, 1997, pp. 35-38; and: *More than a Mirror: How Clients Influence Therapists' Lives* (ed: Marcia Hill) Harrington Park Press, an imprint of The Haworth Press, Inc., 1997, pp. 35-38. Single or multiple copies of this article are available for a fee from The Haworth Document Delivery Service [1-800-342-9678, 9:00 a.m. - 5:00 p.m. (EST). E-mail address: getinfo@haworth.com].

addicts in Montreal, foster families in Vermont, students at a university counseling center, and patients on an acute ward of a state hospital. It was during my work at the health center, however, that I matured as a psychologist and as a person. I believe the two were related. This paper is a brief description of lessons I learned from the health center clients and from my experiences with them.

FOUR LESSONS

Loss of innocence. The first lesson was that people do worse things to each other than I would ever have imagined. Given the circumstances of people I had worked with prior to my experience at the health center, this lesson was not merely a result of my having previously been unusually sheltered. It was, instead, a result of the intimacy that comes with listening to people's stories on a weekly basis, sometimes extending for several years. Two of the stories, in particular, involved traumas suffered at the hands of parents who had been unusually creative in the horrors they inflicted. I listened, attempted to contain much of my shock and revulsion, and had vivid nightmares for months. Later, in work as a volunteer with Amnesty International and as a lawyer for people seeking political asylum, I was exposed to more stories of torture. While I felt anger, sadness and revulsion at these additional stories, I never again felt the shock I experienced when working closely with my clients at the health center.

Triumph of hope. A corollary to the first lesson is that people can be more resilient than I had ever dreamed. I worked with a couple confronted with seemingly insurmountable obstacles who persevered and overcame each obstacle until they had reestablished a strong family life together. I worked with a number of people who overcame early traumas to begin to trust others again. I saw children bravely going on with their peer relationships, school and other activities while trying to cope with the difficulties of divorce. Over time, all of these people dealt with fear, anger, confusion and sadness and emerged happier, with more confidence and pride in their accomplishments. The triumphs of these clients have been inspiring to me both in my work and in my personal life.

Expression of feelings. In the course of my graduate training, I learned to analyze my own feelings for countertransference and to be very careful about the nature and degree of emotions I expressed as a therapist. Integration of my training and instincts came with time and experience. One of the most significant experiences occurred with an adult client who told of physical and emotional abuse she had endured as a child. One day, as she described what she remembered, my eyes filled with tears and some of them rolled down my face. She stopped in mid-sentence and stared at me. When she asked why I was crying, I said that I felt very sad about what had happened to her. The combination of her surprise and my training in containing emotions and analyzing countertransference led to my discussing the case in group supervision. The psychoanalytic supervisor was very upset by my "acting out [my] countertransference" and suggested I seek psychotherapy. This was confusing and upsetting to me, because I believed my reaction had been an appropriate one, under the circumstances. My regular individual supervisor, who was a Sullivanian interpersonal psychologist, supported my interpretation and actions. The ultimate answer came two years later when the therapy was terminated by mutual agreement. I asked the client what aspect of therapy had been most important to her. Without hesitation she said, "when you cried." Sometime in the course of her therapy she told me that if she ever cried when she was a child, she was slapped in the face and told to stop. She had, understandably, learned not to cry or to express many other feelings. My crying gave her two things to think about. First, she realized that what had happened to her was unusual and sad. Second, my crying had freed her to believe that even "normal" people get sad and cry sometimes. Her crying as we said goodbye at the end of therapy freed me to believe that even good therapists can sometimes express their feelings.

The power of therapy. A final lesson was that therapy can be more powerful than I had ever realized. This lesson was derived from experiences with various types of interventions, but the most dramatic example occurred when a health center physician introduced me to a patient who was in her final two weeks of pregnancy. The patient did not believe she was pregnant and refused to allow physicians to examine her. The physicians were concerned both about how the fetus was positioned and about how the woman would cope with labor and delivery.

Two weeks was a time line that eliminated the possibility of most forms of therapy. This was a time-pressured problem with very high stakes and obvious endpoints. Hypnosis was the only treatment I could think of that had the possibility of working that quickly, but I had only used it in situations where I had had several sessions with clients and worked on behavioral problems such as smoking or relaxation. I was anxious about using hypnosis in this situation, but it seemed to be the only option.

Fortunately, the client was hypnotizable. I taught her self-hypnosis and after practicing for a week, she was able to allow a physician to examine her. I taught the physician to help her with self-hypnosis since I did not expect to be present for the delivery.

It worked! I was probably more surprised than anyone else involved.

Years later I learned about relationships between personality variables and hypnotizability that help explain why this was likely to be a good intervention with this particular client. The lesson at the time, however, was to have more confidence in the tools in my toolbox and to hone my skills to use such powerful tools.

My graduate training in clinical psychology taught methods and theories of analysis and intervention to understand and ameliorate problems of clients. It was my ongoing experience with clients at the community health center that eventually made me an effective therapist by presenting me with a broad and seemingly unpredictable variety of client problems, and by teaching me to integrate my training and instincts. As a result of this experience, I developed a richer understanding of the range of challenges people confront across the life span. I also developed an appreciation of the power and variety of resources that we, as people and as therapists, can marshal to cope with those challenges. It was a privilege to be trusted and confided in by my clients and I am grateful to them, my physician colleagues, and an excellent clinical supervisor for the lessons learned.

The Effect of a Therapist's Pregnancy on a Therapeutic Relationship with an Inmate Charged with Infanticide

Maria J. Rivera

SUMMARY. This paper describes the impact of pregnancy on a therapeutic relationship. It is a personal account, told from the therapist's perspective. Specifically, it discusses the effects of the interaction between the increasingly noticeable pregnancy of the clinician, and the circumstances of the patient: an incarcerated woman charged with the death of a toddler. It explores the psychodynamic changes during the course of therapy due to the clinician's pregnancy and the inmate's crime. The therapist describes an increasingly negative countertransference, while the patient expresses an attitude of superiority over the clinician. It is suggested that the patient identified with the therapist and that both members of the therapeutic alliance were dealing with their own internal struggle with their ability to mother. *[Article copies available for a fee from The Haworth Document Delivery Service: 1-800-342-9678. E-mail address: getinfo@haworth.com]*

I was employed as a therapist in a women's correctional facility. Most women there are currently on trial and/or awaiting sentencing. Most are there on drug related charges. There is a small cluster of women who are

The author continues to work with incarcerated women, and is raising a daughter.

Address correspondence to: Maria J. Rivera, PhD, 50 Glenwood Avenue, Jersey City, NJ 07306.

[Haworth co-indexing entry note]: "The Effect of a Therapist's Pregnancy on a Therapeutic Relationship with an Inmate Charged with Infanticide." Rivera, Maria J. Co-published simultaneously in *Women & Therapy* (The Haworth Press, Inc.) Vol. 20, No. 1, 1997, pp. 39-44; and: *More than a Mirror: How Clients Influence Therapists' Lives* (ed: Marcia Hill) Harrington Park Press, an imprint of The Haworth Press, Inc., 1997, pp. 39-44. Single or multiple copies of this article are available for a fee from The Haworth Document Delivery Service [1-800-342-9678, 9:00 a.m. - 5:00 p.m. (EST). E-mail address: getinfo@haworth.com].

there on charges related to the deaths of children, most often their own. The psychiatric clinic had an open door policy, so that any inmate can seek counseling or therapy. Many of the inmates just choose to "ventilate" about the fear of the case.

More often, those inmates who have been charged with a child's death are mandated by the court to seek psychiatric services. Due to the social hierarchy within the jail, these women are segregated from the rest of the prison population. Other inmates see this infanticide as the most heinous crime, and often take justice into their own hands and assault these inmates. Hence these women do not participate in the social protocol dictated by the jail environment. Remarkably, when I have inquired as to whether or not these particular inmates socialized with each other, several have denied it. I treat this information very tentatively, as I am an authority within the system, and most inmates proceed with caution in terms of revealing information about other inmates.

In my tenure at the clinic I had become well known amongst inmates as the "counselor" to talk to about sexual and reproductive issues (e.g., requests for abortion, sexual harassment problems with correction officers). This reputation then led to a more serious issue: women who were in jail for killing children began to seek out my services. While I did not seek this out as a therapeutic interest initially, I became very interested in the psychological and mourning processes that were unique to these women.

I must admit that my observations of these women are based on a very small sample, and my examinations of these women are not within the parameters of true scientific methodology. Nonetheless, there were some marked similarities. All the women who had killed either their own child or one known to them denied their actions in the initial sessions of the therapy. After careful analysis and several sessions, they would admit their actions, but it became evident that they adamantly would deny any intention. That is, none of the women stated that they had premeditated thoughts or plans about killing the child. All of the women (age range 16-34) saw the deaths as a result of an accident (e.g., dying of an asthma attack when accidently left unattended), blamed someone else (e.g., boyfriend), or could not recall the events immediately preceding the child's death. Due to taunting and harassment by other inmates, these women often presented a very stoic exterior in front of others. This emotional detachment was quite noticeable during the initial phase of the therapy. This emotional aloofness was often interpreted as a lack of feeling, which was frequently construed as guilt by inmates and my colleagues. Only after several sessions would the women actually exhibit their feelings about the baby, or their remorse about what happened. All of them reported feeling acute grief and continued reporting feelings that were indic-ative of mourning, all the while maintaining the stance that the death of the child was not deliberate. This array of emotions was only displayed in the therapy sessions. Due to confidentiality and trust issues, clinical staff had little communication with the lawyers and families of these patients, albeit every patient reported overwhelming support from both their lawyers and families.

For the therapist, the internal cognitive and emotional processes are very active and turbulent. Countertransferential issues are marked, and not as unconscious as one might expect. My colleagues made it known that they were unwilling to work with this subpopulation. I suspect these staff members were susceptible to applying a guilty verdict prior to any in-formation. This raises an issue many clinicians in forensics must entertain: whether the psychological explanation for someone's behavior serves as the justification for their behavior, thereby excusing the behavior. Some of my colleagues would then believe that treating these patients and showing empathy implied that they were condoning the inmates' behavior. I myself held the distinction between the explanation and justification in the back of my mind while in session. I was well aware that I had to hold on to this thought with this group of inmates. This was my own way of dealing with the heinous nature of their potential crime.

Much of the therapy that I used with this subpopulation had a feminist social constructionist framework. Using this premise allowed me to offer the empathy that these women needed. I held it in my head that the legal system was biased against women. I was aware that the courts would bestow a more severe punishment on women than on men who committed infanticide. Most of these women were of low economic status, which resulted in poor legal representation, and poor investigation of their cases. Additionally, they described poor relationships with male partners. Hence, I saw these patients as being at a greater disadvantage than the rest of the inmate population.

There was one patient on trial for murder. Briefly, this inmate had custody of her sister's child (the sister was a drug addict). The child was burned in a hot bathtub. The inmate treated what she perceived as a minor burn, and reported that the child's conduct returned to normal. The inmate had judged that since the child had resumed normal playing and eating behavior, the child was not hurt. Four days later, the child began to have seizures. The inmate took the child to the hospital, where he died due to an "internal infection."

The inmate came down to the clinic at the recommendation of her lawyer. According to the inmate, the suggestion was made after the lawyer observed the inmate crying hysterically in court. The patient reported feeling very upset by the taunting of other inmates, who referred to her as "baby killer." She reported hearing this name calling in her sleep and had constant dreams about the child. The initial diagnosis was post-traumatic stress disorder, and adjustment disorder with depressed mood. This was her first incarceration. In the initial session, the patient basically described her symptoms and her case. This patient viewed the death as an accident, and saw it as a result of her ignorance and negligence. She described how the hot water would surge in her apartment, and she did not consider this when she left the child in the tub to bathe. She believed the child was fine since he had resumed playing and eating. The patient pointed out that she did take the baby to the hospital, which was evidence that she did not want the child to die. Letters of support were written to the judge by everyone in the family and community.

In subsequent sessions, the patient revealed that the death of this child was particularly difficult since she had custody of him since birth. In addition, she had just had a second trimester miscarriage, a pregnancy that she wanted desperately. She had two children (ages 11 and 7) from her first husband. The lost pregnancy resulted from her relationship with her current long-term boyfriend. She had to take parenting classes in order to obtain custody of her nephew; this was an added burden of guilt for her.

During one session, she spoke about her sister (her nephew's mother), and the hatred she had for her. Close in age, the two were rivals very early on. The patient described herself as the good seed and her sister was the bad seed. The sister was described as a burden to the family due to her drug habit. The patient frequently cried about how the sister hurt and used their mother. The sister stole from the mother to supply her drug habit, and had abandoned her other five children at the mother's home. The sister did not attend her child's funeral. It was uncertain if the sister even knew that her child had died, for no one had seen her in several months.

During the course of treatment with this inmate, I became pregnant. I made the decision not to discuss the pregnancy unless it became an issue during the treatment. Interestingly, it became an underlying focus of the treatment, yet this patient would never discuss the issue directly when questioned. As soon as I began to show, she insisted that I was having a boy. Interestingly, the quality of the sessions changed when the patient became aware that this would be my first child. Prior to this, she would always come in, emoting, tearful and eager to discuss her experience. After, she became the expert in the sessions. She would come in providing advice and telling me what to expect with a child and pregnancy. She pointed out on several occasions what she learned in her parenting classes.

She ignored the fact that I was the staff member who ran a group for pregnant inmates. If other inmates asked me questions regarding my pregnancy, this patient would respond to the question. It became very difficult to return the focus of the sessions to her. When I mentioned this change in focus, the inmate would either deny this, or completely avoid the issue.

As my pregnancy progressed, my thinking and behavior began to change about this patient. I began to question her innocence, and I could no longer rely on using a feminist framework to help supply empathy. I began to become annoyed at her when she would advise me on child rearing. I was not upset that she was not focusing on the therapy. Rather, due to my own countertransferential issues, I was angry at her for trying to tell me what to do. *"After all, she has only taken a six-week course, and I am a psychologist."* I was struggling to avoid thinking the worst, but the thought was lurking in my mind; *"How dare you, I'm not in jail for killing a baby."* I was unable to explain the anger I was experiencing, but it manifested itself in my feeling very protective over my pregnancy. I no longer wanted it as the focus of the sessions, and tried to clarify this on several occasions. I was uncertain if this anger was due to my unconscious response to the patient's crime, or whether, unconsciously, I was becoming fearful that since I was pregnant, she might hurt me. I felt as if the therapy had become competitive, behaviorally and emotionally, and I became less involved with the patient. I would not struggle to maintain her appointments, given the correction officers' unwillingness to escort the patient to the clinic. I would feel regret on the days that I would have to meet with her, or I would be eager to conclude a session.

I was unable to objectively analyze this experience for several reasons. Due to staff changes, I did not have a supervisor at the time. In addition, the patient was transferred abruptly to a different correctional facility. I do know that this case, as well as my pregnancy, has greatly affected my professional abilities. I have become more aware of my limitations as a therapist, specifically with the realization of how my personal life can and will intrude upon treatment. The other change has been that I'm more cautious and alert about taking on the cases of women who commit infanticide. I find myself less eager to believe or empathize with them. The internal struggle that I go through is much more evident.

Retrospectively, I find myself feeling disappointed that I was unable to maintain a clinically objective stance. My negative feelings for this patient, and my protective feelings for my pregnancy were so overwhelming, that I do not believe I served this patient well. I believe that some of my own personal issues did interfere. When this patient began telling me what to do as a parent, this raised certain conflicts that I had with my own mother, as well as exacerbated the fears that I had about my abilities as a parent. I also believe that since this was my first pregnancy, my anxiety and fears increased my overprotective view. As far as my changing belief that the patient was guilty, I believe this came about as a way to control the session, and as a way of expressing my own rage against her efforts to control the session, and because my prospective methods of parenting were being questioned.

I was unable to see that her efforts to control the session and her suggestions for parenting were more than just an effort to "control" me. I do believe that these behaviors had the unconscious "function" of improving her own destroyed self-image as a woman and mother. She also needed to alleviate some of the guilt over the death of her nephew; hence she felt that I was having a boy, and this would undo the crime. I do believe that this woman identified with me as a pregnant woman, since she had recently had a second trimester miscarriage. I now believe that her forceful suggestions about parenting were a way to prove to herself that she was a good mother, despite being charged with the murder of a baby.

If I were able to do things differently, I do think I would have addressed the impact of my pregnancy more overtly, given the nature of the patient's crime and her own recent miscarriage. I would have paid attention to my own anxiety and feelings, with the goal of eventually incorporating them into the session. Retrospectively, I now see that both the patient and I were responding to our own feelings about our ability to be a mother, albeit for different reasons. Had I addressed these feelings in the session, I believe that I would have been a better therapist for her.

Happy, Happy, Happy

Ellen Cole

SUMMARY. In this article the author reflects on her upbringing, in which she was admonished to be cheerful and happy and not acknowledge unpleasantness. Consequently, as a young adult and a new psychotherapist she found herself detached from her own feelings as well as those of her clients. She recalls the evening that she became a more whole, more sensitive human being, and credits her therapy practice and her clients for keeping her that way. *[Article copies available for a fee from The Haworth Document Delivery Service: 1-800-342-9678. E-mail address: getinfo@haworth.com]*

"Don't say anything unless you have something nice to say." My first lesson. From my smiling, ever-cheerful mother. The same mother whose brother died of cancer in his late 30s, the same mother who told my brother, my father, and me, "If I ever get cancer, I don't want to know." The same mother who contracted uterine cancer in her 50s after taking the large daily dose of unopposed estrogen that was the regimen of choice for menopausal women in the early 1970s. And my good father did *not* tell my mother that she had cancer. He didn't tell her, he didn't tell my brother, and he didn't tell me. My mother kept on smiling, believing she was undergoing radiation therapy for a "pre-cancerous condition."

Ellen Cole, PhD, is Professor of Psychology at Alaska Pacific University. She co-edits The Haworth Press's book program, "Innovations in Feminist Studies," co-hosts a call-in radio show in Anchorage, and conducts a small sex therapy practice.

Address correspondence to: Dr. Ellen Cole, Alaska Pacific University, 4101 University Drive, Anchorage, AK 99508.

[Haworth co-indexing entry note]: "Happy, Happy, Happy." Cole, Ellen. Co-published simultaneously in *Women & Therapy* (The Haworth Press, Inc.) Vol. 20, No. 1, 1997, pp. 45-48; and: *More than a Mirror: How Clients Influence Therapists' Lives* (ed: Marcia Hill) Harrington Park Press, an imprint of The Haworth Press, Inc., 1997, pp. 45-48. Single or multiple copies of this article are available for a fee from The Haworth Document Delivery Service [1-800-342-9678, 9:00 a.m. - 5:00 p.m. (EST). E-mail address: getinfo@haworth.com].

I remember when I was very little being pinched on the cheek by my uncle who ordered me to "stop pouting." (Just this morning–50 years later–I found myself apologizing because my feet hurt after a tennis game, and I didn't feel like smiling.)

As a young adult and a new mother I moved to Vermont. My parents continued to live in New York City, and we talked on the phone every Sunday. My mother told me she didn't want to hear bad news, only good news. If I or the babies had a cold, please don't tell her; she'd worry too much.

My brother, younger by four years, was and is on the moody side. He stayed in his room a lot when we were kids. I, by contrast, had the job of being the cheerful daughter, not particularly well-behaved, but smart in school, outgoing, and of course always smiling.

To this day my 80-year-old Mom begins our still weekly telephone conversations by saying, "Ellen, you're so up. It makes me so happy to talk to you." My 81-year-old Dad admonishes me, from time to time, to "cheer down." I play my role as cheerleader well, and I must say, I actually enjoy it. I'm glad I got this script and not another.

But I recall the day my armor showed a chink, and it first entered my consciousness that there may be something more to life, to my life, than this one-dimensional sense of always needing to be happy. It was in 1972, a beautiful summer day in Vermont, and I was sitting around a picnic table with a bunch of other pre-school moms, watching our kids play by the bank of a lake. We started to share our feelings about this and that. One woman was angry at her husband, another was sad over the loss of a family pet. I had no feelings. Not a clue. Empty.

I had by then earned a Master's degree in Counseling Psychology, had started a university counseling center, had seen many clients, and was just beginning a doctoral program. I was no stranger to feelings, as long as they weren't my own. And even then, my approach to my clients was detached, unemotional. I didn't feel my own feelings, and I certainly didn't feel their's.

Several weeks later I attended my Monday night women's group. Our format was to spend the first hour as a big group and then break into pairs for personal sharing. Until that night I was very reserved in the group. (Then, I thought of myself as being "together"; now I realize I was just "out of touch" with my issues.) I rarely had any problems to share, although I was a good listener, cheerful and concerned.

That particular night ended the week from hell. My husband was in England, leaving me to milk seven cows twice a day by myself, take care of two young children, and go to work as usual every day. On the way to my women's group I was stopped by a cop and ticketed for running a stop sign. Emotionally and physically exhausted, I burst into tears when I sat down with my listening partner. I sobbed, and I talked. I felt miserable. And then I felt better. I couldn't believe it. Do you mean it's possible to be a smart, strong woman and be vulnerable in a semi-public setting? It's okay to shed a tear and actually feel better afterward? To admit my life was less than perfect? That I couldn't handle it all? It's okay to pout? I don't have to be cheerful? I don't have to smile? Oh my god.

It was that evening that I became a therapist in more than training. Once I was able to be vulnerable myself, I began to love my clients in a new way, to appreciate their bravery and courage. And it was a circle. As I more intentionally invited the shadows and uncertainties of my clients into the therapy session, I began to feel more comfortable with my own human fallibility.

I am a college teacher and an editor and an all-around (basically happy and cheerful) busy person. I do not have to be a psychotherapist. It's not my major source of income, nor has it ever really been the mainstay of my career. But I keep a hand in. I always see a few clients at a time, and I think I know why. It is only partly for altruistic reasons, because I believe I am helpful to people. It is only partly because I have a skill and feel satisfaction at doing what I do well. It is only partly because I am a detective at heart, and I love a good, soulful story. It is only partly because, as a teacher of graduate counseling students, I believe I need to practice what I teach. *And* it is also because I *need* to see clients. I need to be reminded that vulnerability and imperfection are integral to the human condition. That when we look at our dark side we are better people, not worse. When I show compassion and understanding to a client, I show it to myself. When a client expresses pain, or shame, or grief, I acknowledge and experience my own. I honor my clients for their authenticity; I honor myself for mine. Judith Jordan (1995) takes this experience a step further, and she says it perfectly:

> . . . I'd rather be in a good therapy session than in almost any social situation I can imagine . . . At its best therapy is about helping people come into their most real and deep places. That is true for both therapist and client . . . And in those places of personal truth, I think we are most clearly connected to a sense of the universal. (p. 271)

Without my therapy practice I might forget that life is–that I am– richer, deeper, more complex than happy, happy, happy. As much as I am able to let them, my clients keep me whole.

REFERENCE

Jordan, Judith V. (1995). Female therapists and the search for a new paradigm. In Michael Sussman (Ed.), *A perilous calling: The hazards of psychotherapy practice.* New York: John Wiley & Sons.

Death Work:
One Psychotherapist's Journey

Marcia Perlstein

SUMMARY. One psychotherapist describes the complex matrix of learning, loss, emotional price, and intense connection experienced in over two decades of working with large numbers of clients who were dying. This article offers a look at one psychotherapist's spiral into depression as the difficult aspects of the work take over and her subsequent movement back to former functioning. The notion of expanding the walls of the psychotherapy office to include others in the work such as members of family of origin, partner in a primary relationship, extended family and close friends, is explored. *[Article copies available for a fee from The Haworth Document Delivery Service: 1-800-342-9678. E-mail address: getinfo@haworth.com]*

I don't know quite when it began; but it cumulatively crept up on me. I'd been working with dying clients for many many years; though when I

Marcia Perlstein, MFCC, has been a practicing psychotherapist in Berkeley, California since 1967. She is currently Director of Psychotherapy Services, North Berkeley Psychiatric Institute and Clinical Director of the Alternative Family Project, San Francisco, CA.

This article is dedicated to "the committee": Karen, Joan, Sylvie, Nyla who helped the author shift the lens; and to the memories of those she has accompanied on their passages; and to others involved in this work who are putting the pieces back together.

All the names in this article, with the exception of the author's mentor Richard Olney, have been changed to protect the confidentiality of the people mentioned.

Address correspondence to: Marcia Perlstein, 1806 Martin Luther King, Jr. Way, Berkeley, CA 94709; e-mail (scraggs3@ccnet.com)

[Haworth co-indexing entry note]: "Death Work: One Psychotherapist's Journey." Perlstein, Marcia. Co-published simultaneously in *Women & Therapy* (The Haworth Press, Inc.) Vol. 20, No. 1, 1997, pp. 49-59; and: *More than a Mirror: How Clients Influence Therapists' Lives* (ed: Marcia Hill) Harrington Park Press, an imprint of The Haworth Press, Inc., 1997, pp. 49-59. Single or multiple copies of this article are available for a fee from The Haworth Document Delivery Service [1-800-342-9678, 9:00 a.m. - 5:00 p.m. (EST). E-mail address: getinfo@haworth.com].

began in the mid-seventies, these clients were only a small percentage of my caseload. By 1995, when I grew quite depressed, my work in this arena had increased a great deal, as had the impact on me. While I have no regrets about any of the clinical/psychosocial work I've done in the area of death and dying, I wish to share both the learnings (professional and personal), the "gifts" from the work and some of the emotional costs as well.

THE FIRST

In 1975, I helped a feisty, irreverent woman in her mid-eighties die at home. She had her adult son call me from the hospital to tell me she wouldn't be able to come to her session because she'd had a heart attack. The next day when I called the hospital, I was able to talk with her. I asked her what I could do; she said, "spring me from here. I know I'm dying but I want to die at home." The therapy was a blend of case management and advocacy. This woman knew what she wanted; she had no trouble with self-esteem or empowerment issues. She was smart enough to enlist me as a professional who could help her translate her desires to the medical establishment; to people who, especially in those days, were accustomed to trying extraordinary measures to keep patients alive. Often these medical gymnastics prolonged patients' lives very little and were extremely intrusive, time consuming and painful. More importantly, this woman chose not to spend her last days engaged in medical procedures; she preferred to have the time with her loved ones. Since there wasn't yet much public education along these lines, there weren't many social supports for a patient being in charge of the medical decisions which affected her life and, ultimately, death.

I had been working, since 1967, in the precious environment of my psychotherapy office. In my clinical training I'd learned about "holding the container." Simultaneously, I'd been active in the community, especially in the women's movement. We had just held a Women's Mental Health Workers Conference which drew over 1,000 lay practitioners and professionals–all called workers. I was quick to accept this client's invitation to bring the office to her hospital and then to her home. I felt I could finally wed my two worlds: professional training and political activism. I rolled up my sleeves and plunged into the Jane Addams Hull House model of hands-on case management and family therapy. I helped translate her wishes to the medical personnel and her somewhat frightened and skeptical adult children (who were older than me). Then I stepped back so she could have the peaceful closings she desired with her family and friends.

They worked out a schedule of brief visits. She died peacefully, in her sleep, within two weeks. If there is such a thing as a "good death," Dorothy's was good. She was where she wanted to be, surrounded by those she most wanted with her. Her bed looked out at the garden she'd lovingly tended for over forty years.

I was asked to come by several hours after she had died. Her eldest daughter and I stood in the vestibule just outside her bedroom, exchanging hushed memories and funny stories characterizing her unique energy and implacability, her unwavering support for the people and issues she cared about. Her memorial service was held in the backyard where everyone felt her presence looking at the event from her bedroom window.

While death is sad, a "good death" leaves people feeling complete. I felt privileged to have known this woman and satisfied that my interventions had helped her operationalize her wishes. I was deeply moved by the entire experience.

And Then

Within the year, I helped a client and her husband with his "home death" from cancer. This was a bit harder. He was a man in his forties, known for his political work. The community was stunned. I was asked to meet with groups of his friends as well as with him and his wife. He railed at the unfairness of it all and fought the good fight until the end. It was extremely painful to see him in such physical and emotional distress.

I continued being called in periodically, through the eighties and to the present, for other deaths. While each one is extremely sad, given the fact of not having choice over the outcome (all would prefer healthy longer lives), when people exercise genuine choice over the "how," there are intense connections between the dying person and each "helper" as well as among the helpers as we participate in the process. I have sometimes felt a deep and profound sense of why I am on this earth.

As the years progressed, public education, the seminal work of Elizabeth Kubler Ross, the growth of the hospice movement, and the organizing of many communities in the arenas of AIDS and cancer added scores of lay people and professionals to participate in this work.

East Bay Volunteer Therapist AIDS Project

By the mid 1980s, I had personally begun to be impacted by the AIDS epidemic, through the painful, ravaging deaths of very close friends. As a civilian, I brought what I had learned in my work to the bedsides of people dear to me. After one of my closest friend's brother died, I made the decision to bring some of my learnings directly to the community. First I joined the San Francisco Volunteer Therapist AIDS Project, which is based on a simple model of licensed psychotherapists and interns receiving training in AIDS work; in exchange for the training they agree to see one client who is HIV positive, at no fee. I began with one client, then two, and then, in the course of several years, many many more. I then decided that I needed to try to recruit other therapists in my community both because many cared and would want to help and because I was beginning to burn out. In Fall of 1989, I founded a similar project named the East Bay Volunteer Therapist AIDS Project (EBVTAP).

We kicked off our project with a training for more than fifty therapists. They ranged from supervised interns to "veterans" with more than forty years of clinical experience. We invited AIDS Project of the East Bay (a local, grass roots multi-service organization) to be our co-sponsoring agency. Thus, as our clients progress in the disease, their volunteer therapists are current with resources available to them, their significant others and families.

THE WAY I LEARNED TO WORK:
CLINICAL TRAINING REVISITED AND REVISED

I have always felt that it was an accident of time that I was seated in the therapist's chair and the client was on the couch. An hour later I might be on my own therapist's couch. This concept resonates in a particular way in working with dying clients: at some point, my turn will come to have people there for me doing what I'm doing in the moment. I think any clinical contributions in this area are quite similar to positive work in any psychotherapy situation with the major difference that time is collapsed in an inverse telescopic fashion. In working with the dying there often isn't the luxury of time to allow insights to evolve gradually and for action to follow slowly. For example, if a client wants to make an attempt at reaching out to those she/he is estranged from, wants to let go of toxic relationships which deplete her energy, sooner is usually better than later.

I have somewhat of an irreverence, though certainly an understanding, of the need for most clinical canon. I support the notion of boundaries, keeping the office safe and sacred as a specially contained environment. However, in working with the dying, I feel permission to throw away the rule book. An example follows:

Tom's HIV had progressed to full blown AIDS. In the past year he had alienated virtually all of his closest friends. The time had come where he needed more and more help, physically, in managing on a daily basis. He acknowledged that he had been extremely hard on his friends and was responsible for their leaving. He wanted a way to tell them so but didn't have the energy for an intense discussion with each one.

He jokingly said that there was probably a group out there of people recovering from his treatment of them. I took him literally and said, "Why don't we work with that group? Let's bring them all in." He laughed, then realized I was quite serious. Slowly he began to smile as the idea, taken seriously, began to become genuinely appealing. I asked him to pull out his address book and give me a guest list replete with names and phone numbers. As he pulled out each name he had a story to tell with the recurring theme of his temper tantrums, critical attitude, and final showdown punctuating each tale. I called nine friends and invited them to my office for an evening the following week. Each one's response was a bit different. I could tell by a particular kind of shock expressed by a few, that they were clients in traditional, boundaried psychotherapy situations. Some were curious. All cared very much about Tom but were wary about getting too close. All of these reactions notwithstanding, every one of them showed up.

When we began, Tom surprised all of us, including me, by acknowledging that he was a "handful," apologizing for driving them away and telling them quite simply that he needed them badly and was very scared. When he went on to say that his worst fear was dying alone, he broke down in quiet sobs. The room was very still. One at a time, each person spoke, pledging to "be there for him."

I told them that it wasn't going to be easy; that not only could they expect increasing physical deterioration, but that Tom would very likely push them away again. The challenge, given what just happened and everybody's commitment to be there, was to find a way to support each other when times got tough with Tom. Some had been through other deaths and knew exactly what I meant. They began organizing a schedule for tasks and time with Tom. They exchanged phone numbers with each other. I suggested they plan a time to meet without me, two weeks down the line, to refine and revise what they had setup after trying it out for awhile. There was a great deal of competence, caring and humor in that room. That night, Tom left with his buddies. The next time he arrived at my office for his individual session he told me that one of his friends who had driven him to the appointment was in the waiting room, ready to take him to the park afterward.

This vignette is merely a small part of the work which preceded and followed it, but it does illustrate a loosening of boundaries in service of the goals. In working with the dying I have brought the office to homes and hospital; just as in the example above and numerous others, the walls of the office have stretched to accommodate many different configurations of groups, extended/blended families, significant others, families of origin. In the best case scenarios, "it takes a village" to help someone in the final stages of life.

Thus, I continued to learn that working with the dying was similar in many regards to traditional work and different, perhaps in format and time frame. I wanted to help these clients, as I would any other, feel empowered; expand their repertoire of personal choices; learn to get in touch with needs and wants rather than shoulds and oughts; translate these learnings into concrete action. Intuitively, many of these clients understood.

I also found that I needed another skill which never came up in any of my clinical training and which I was unprepared to develop: speaking at memorial services. Especially in AIDS work, families of origin are often in other parts of the country. They come together in various ways, often into my office, at time of diagnosis. Each person has a unique and complicated set of issues to confront. Many are coming out about being gay or lesbian at the same time as they are telling their families they are HIV positive. People are now living longer than they were when I began this work. At first, many died in under a year. When families came out for the last weeks of an adult son or daughter's life, their contact with the community of friends, significant others, and therapist was very intense. We were one of the first projects in our area to offer services to women with AIDS. Many of our initial female clients were mothers and had to make difficult decisions about telling their children and planning for their eventual adoption. We were often able to help them bring together the resources of many different agencies as we became a kind of "home room," a place from which they could go forth with support.

One of our volunteer therapists began a mothers' group for local women; the group members always welcomed visiting moms for whatever period of time out-of-state moms were in the area. One woman from a southern state who had come to California without her husband (since he had disowned their son and forbade her to tell folks back home what their son was dying of) felt closer to the other mothers in the group than to friends of over forty years, since she could name the disease, ask specific questions, and experience some very difficult feelings openly, with others going through their own versions of preparing for their adult sons' deaths.

One of the mothers from the group picked her up at the airport, found her a room in someone's house, brought her to group sessions. In between face-to-face meetings she spoke on the phone with others in the group and called upon them as needed. Meanwhile, her son was working with his volunteer therapist to make decisions about how he wanted to die. One of the most poignant examples of mindful preparation occurred when his mother first arrived at his apartment. In the weeks preceding her arrival, he had given away all his possessions that had any meaning to him, leaving in his room a few prized items to look at. Since he was bedridden, he had some friends remove all his clothes. He asked them to leave, however, hanging in the closet, three flannel shirts. When his mother arrived, he said that he thought she might get chilly and that all she needed to do was open the closet door, warmth was waiting for her.

The memorial service was a lifeline to this grieving mother. By hearing from his significant other, friends, and therapist, she was able to get a feeling for the happinesses in his life and a glimpse at some of his many contributions. She was brought up-to-date with the life he had led since he had left home. Members of her group brought her to the service and sat with her throughout.

For me, as the therapist, I experienced much of what many others have reported who work with dying clients. I felt a deep human connection, not only to each client, but to his family and friends; the AIDS community; and, often, by extension, to humankind. There was a way that people nurtured each other, made themselves available for the most basic levels of care, that one would wish could occur as a matter of course in people's ordinary lives and dealings with each other. Then, in contrast, there were terribly painful experiences such as one client's dementia which frightened friends and family and drove people away; and several clients with families of origin who were critical and judgmental and would not be present. I had to find ways to locate other resources so that too much of the emotional work would not fall on my own shoulders. Sometimes that is easier said than done. I took more horror stories home with me than I could ultimately absorb.

Civilian Deaths

In this period, I suffered the loss of close friends my own age (one from AIDS, another two from cancer, another from a sudden brain aneurism) and a mentor. I was invited to be part of a team to help Richard Olney, founder of Self Acceptance Training, with his dying process at his home in

Milwaukee. While being of assistance, my attention was always where it was most needed, on the dying person, family, and friends. I hadn't the time to notice how the losses began to wear me down. In the intensity of each process I had lost track of myself; very poor modelling for any therapist to say nothing of the gradual harm to myself.

EMOTIONAL BUILD-UP

My growing despondency crept up on me slowly; I was not aware of it for a very long time. It wasn't merely the problematical cases that caused me pain; the cumulative effect of even the so called "good deaths" wore away at me. I became overwhelmed with sadness over the deaths of people whom I'd come to know and love. The loss of young people in their twenties, thirties, forties, and fifties, reversing the natural order of things, the way it was "supposed to be" as they predeceased their parents, always saddened me in each individual instance; and whenever I thought about the numbers and the statistics, I became not just saddened, but often enraged and overwhelmed.

From a gregarious person, I became one who needed more and more time alone; encouraging even friends to call me at my office, craving silence when I was home. I found myself gaining weight, exercising not at all, reading little and zoning out to TV when I wasn't actually working with people. I was in denial about my own physical symptoms, which needed attention, for fear that "no news was good news"; I harbored the notion that if I went to the doctor I'd find out I had a fatal disease. A pimple became cancer, tiredness signalled AIDS. I was diagnosed with diabetes and did have an arrhythmia. I resented the time I had to spend on my own health including visits to my internist and cardiologist, time spent monitoring my own blood pressure and glucose levels.

I took longer and longer to answer calls which were not AIDS related. I begged off social invitations, feeling too tired. My significant other and I stopped having events which had become rituals among our chosen extended family, such as Hanukkah, Christmas eve and sedar. I also had a form of survivor guilt. Why was I still alive while all these other folks, many much younger than I, were gone? I had something of a spiritual dilemma over the issue of why. I couldn't understand how there could be a larger meaning to all the pain and sadness. The child in me decided God was definitely not a woman: no woman would mess things up so badly. I cried many times during the day, often having to "get myself together" when the light lit up indicating a client was in the waiting room. I finally turned to a psychiatrist colleague and friend who prescribed antidepressants.

My Community Rallies

Fortunately, I signalled my growing crisis in a serendipitous way. I found out that my significant other and friends, a year in advance, were already planning a large surprise birthday party for my fiftieth. I found myself crying and dreading the event, far away though it was. I couldn't imagine enjoying myself when so many people had died. I was becoming so upset in advance that I had to tell a few key people that I'd found out and that I didn't want them to go forward with the planning. When some indicated that I might feel differently, I told them that if they continued I would plan to be on the East Coast and not show up; that was how frightened I was at the prospect of trying not to cry at my own party. They finally heard me about a large party.

However, my loving and creative friends, undeterred and unbeknownst to me (they were successful at the herculean task of keeping me in the dark), organized a massive effort to celebrate me without a party. A core group comprised of three of my closest friends and my significant other, found over two hundred of my nearest and dearest family and friends, from across the country and in every category of my life: family, teaching, political activism, college, graduate school, neighbors, ex-lovers, extended family replete with adults and young children, colleagues.

They set up shooting schedules over a three-month period; the filmmaker edited all the material inserting photographs and shots of the ocean, my office, our home, my dog, etc., with the spoken words of all the people they had located. They used a motif of a heart which a textile artist friend of the filmmaker designed, and added an original soundtrack created by my filmmaker friend's partner. They honored my wishes not to have a surprise party. Instead, the "committee" as they had come to be known, presented *Marcia: The Mini-Series* to me on the actual day of my fiftieth birthday. In finished form it ran four hours. We viewed a chunk of it together, then my partner and I went off to the city; finally, that evening we had a small, very carefully planned party with the extended families, including most of the children in my life.

With a Video in Me

The video had a result far beyond what any of the planners could have dreamt. Something inside me snapped and my burnout, distress, and depression all lifted. It was as though all the people who loved and appreciated me gave me a huge spiritual shot of adrenalin that soared through my system and lifted me from a very tunneled, narrow perspective and back into a larger, more fully encompassing reality. Though on celluloid, they spoke to me as though they were all standing beside me. I began to see that I could choose a more life-affirming way of living even as I helped the dying. My life remained the same in that I continued directing the AIDS project as well as all my other professional commitments. What shifted, however, was my emotional relationship to everything I was doing. What lifted was my social isolation. I wanted to spend time with everyone, to make more memories. I began working in walks and lunches with friends, theater, movies, having people over. I favored frequent shorter contacts, rather than waiting for the harder-to-schedule lengthy, open-ended times. I began looking forward to the ring of the phone. In short, I was back to myself. I shifted the lens so that the main focus in my life became the living. I tapped into my appreciation of the people in my life. I began to delegate more; and when people were dying, I helped, but played a less central role. I took more and longer vacations from four-day weekends to an eleven-day trip to New York (the longest I'd been there since relocating to California in 1965!). Now I find that I'm once again working harder, but I'm fueling the additional work with lots more play as well. My energy is back to its legendary level, motivated by the joy I take in the things I do and the people in my life. I've been off antidepressants since about one week after my fiftieth birthday.

When anyone asks what made the difference, I say, "I have a video in me." And most importantly, I am acutely aware of how precious feeling good can be; how lucky I am. I am vigilant about slippage and will use one of a myriad of stress reduction techniques such as meditation, a hot bath, a walk, or even simple breathing exercises when the pressure starts building.

AND NOW

In May of 1996, I accepted the Clinical Directorship of the Alternative Family Project. Friends and colleagues were aghast that I added to my workload. I see it as continuing the changes I began in moving towards life, while continuing to help in the death and dying arena. This project is about families and children in the gay, lesbian, bisexual and transsexual community. It is about celebrating life while developing tools for coping with complex issues that beset all families, with added pressures on alternative ones. Acceptance of this position has meant cutting back on work in the AIDS project with an eye towards phasing it out by 1999 (ten years after founding EBVTAP).

For colleagues without the "video solution" available to them I would recommend breaking isolation and reaching out to peers, close friends and family. Even if it feels as though you don't have the energy for complicated social contacts, short and somewhat frequent one-on-one walks, coffee, phone conversations are essential. Let others in when they reach out to you. Consider seeking focused professional help; someone with a bit of distance often can help you see what you may have overlooked. Occasional long weekends, drives into the country, vacations away from phones, offices, hospitals and homes are essential. Find pockets of quiet time by yourself. Make the time for experiences which uplift and inspire you such as in nature, art and music. The most important thing is to recognize your slippage as it is occurring and allow yourself all the time you need for refueling.

Now the glass is, once again, half full. I have done what many others in the field of death and dying have done, translated a good deal of the work in the field into tools for living a more mindful life. I've learned perspective, not to "sweat the small stuff." I'm a slightly gentler, more patient version of my former self. I appreciate aspects of my dailiness in a different way, from lifting the shades in the morning and looking outside, to evening walks, quiet moments with the newspaper, the sounds of children playing on the street.

Now the uneventful is a blessing. I treasure the mundane. For who knows when my time will come? Until then, I hope I can continue contributing in a way which isn't as costly to my own mental health as I once had allowed it to be.

Mystical Experience of a Counsellor: An Autobiographical Journey

Catherine Racine

SUMMARY. The recent emergence of mystical experience in psychological literature and the burgeoning of spirituality within mainstream counselling are beginning to challenge many assumptions on which the field of counselling psychology is precariously perched. Mystical experience itself is being reported by significant numbers of clients, and a developing theory describes it as a positive and transforming phenomenon. However, there is a notable absence of therapists' voices regarding mystical experience which needs to be addressed if we are to be accountable to our clients, our peers, and ourselves. Using my own voice and a personal anecdote from my thesis on mystical experience, I examine this contentious and enigmatic experience to illuminate some significant issues it has raised for me. *[Article copies available for a fee from The Haworth Document Delivery Service: 1-800-342-9678. E-mail address: getinfo@haworth.com]*

I had an experience in the summer of 1993 that was so extraordinary, from my perspective as a counsellor in training, that I decided to make it the focus of my Master's thesis. The process that led to this decision, and that

Catherine Racine is a feminist counsellor, writer, and educator, who has recently completed her MA in counselling psychology at the University of British Columbia, Canada.

Please address correspondence to: Catherine Racine, 6311 Spender Drive, Richmond, British Columbia, Canada VFE 4B9.

[Haworth co-indexing entry note]: "Mystical Experience of a Counsellor: An Autobiographical Journey." Racine, Catherine. Co-published simultaneously in *Women & Therapy* (The Haworth Press, Inc.) Vol. 20, No. 1, 1997, pp. 61-68; and: *More than a Mirror: How Clients Influence Therapists' Lives* (ed: Marcia Hill) Harrington Park Press, an imprint of The Haworth Press, Inc., 1997 pp. 61-68. Single or multiple copies of this article are available for a fee from The Haworth Document Delivery Service [1-800-342-9678, 9:00 a.m. - 5:00 p.m. (EST). E-mail address: getinfo@haworth.com].

has unfolded since then, has been so rich and convoluted that it bears more resemblance to a discovery than a choice. Indeed, my process tracks a remarkable journey into a new world where I am no longer the hapless scribe of my own experience, but rather the budding author of my own life.

The experience I am about to describe was not really new to me at all, as I later realized in recounting my own life stories for what became an autobiographical study on mystical experience. Yet the intensity, the fantastic beauty, the fierce joy and longing that this experience engendered, shattered the boundaries of my professional equanimity as a counsellor in training. I have questioned those boundaries ever since.

The event occurred during a practice counselling session with a student from one of my classes in the Counselling Psychology program. The session was part of a larger project requiring class members to interview briefly a classmate to determine which tests would be best suited to the stated concerns of a client. My "client," whom I shall call Chris, was an unobtrusive man I had spoken to only briefly in a course we had taken together 18 months earlier. In our second class together, we briefly exchanged our views on community and its central importance in our lives during what was ostensibly a 10-minute counselling session. I was interested to discover he had considerable experience living and working in a spiritual community and was keen to hear more. Other than these brief encounters I knew little of the man, although I was aware he was a reserved individual who expressed himself reticently in class– and towards whom I felt a small collegial bond.

To break the monotony of the day, Chris and I had decided to conduct the interview outside in the Nitobe Gardens–a Japanese garden on campus–after our morning class. Because the day was overcast and rainy, we ended up sitting in a rain shelter overlooking the pond. The interview, which was to last 15 to 20 minutes, went on for an hour and a half during which time I experienced a profound encounter with this client, as the following story describes.

THE THIRD THING

You're talking, I see your lips move and hear the sound, but my mind is running. For what? For shelter, for validation, for a reason, for joy. I feel my mind turning over like a car with a dead battery, stalled, while an unseen driver intently turns the key, turns the key, turns the key. I am struggling to remember the name of your sister, your brother, the details of what happened. I want to hang on to the details, I'm supposed to have them in mind, but I can't. There is only You, only You and this dawning ecstasy.

Some part of me races down the corridors of memory, opening doors, checking contents, searching, rifling through files looking for the match to this experience. But I know what's happening, of course I know. I know what's happening and I don't dare believe it. I'm so afraid my hope will kill this, that the moment will dissolve like a mirage before my thirsty soul, and abandon me like a broken promise. This can not be happening, I'll try to ignore it, pretend it isn't there. But it is. Holy God it is.

Gazing down at my arms I see my skin spiked with gooseflesh, I feel the hairs standing at attention, tuned to this impossible moment. The moment endures past my fear, I dare breath, I can trust it, can't I? This feeling is everywhere around us, but mostly here, the source is here, in this rain shelter, where he speaks while I listen. Where the rain falls in a mist around us, smudging the edges and filling all the in-betweens with something that loves me, all of me, and that I love in return with an inundating gratitude that longs to express itself in great wracking sobs.

Does he know what's happening? How can he not? He offers no clue but the words keep coming, and the story opens like a rose, petal by petal. I yearn towards its center as a flower leans towards the light. With each word, each poetic pause, each gesture, he becomes more naked, more precious, the wounds and scars more clearly defined and dear. I wonder if he will undress down to his bones. The parade unreels like a film behind my eyes. I see the people he describes, meet his family members, walk through their home, stroll around his town. I endure the indignities, the penury, the loss, the unbearable loss.

What can I offer him for his pain? What? Empathy? Guidance? For what? For his gift? For the joy? The sight? For his sacred story? What can I offer? Nothing. Nothing.

My body riots behind a seamless composure. I clench my teeth to keep them from chattering. A fist expands in my throat and aches with a need to cry. No, no, no, no. Finally tears break through the barrier and sit on my eyes blinding and burning me. I tip my head back to keep them from spilling down my face, but there are too many waiting for release. I brush them away with the back of my hand pretending my eyes are tired and want to be rubbed. "Are you cold?" he asks me. I don't know, am I? "No I'm fine, please go on," someone with my voice responds.

What has seeped into my pores now thunders through me like a mountain cascade. I adore him, his unbearable perfection, the angel wings hidden from view but surely there, the golden cadence of his voice, the fine milky skin on his forehead, his heroic fear. I have to celebrate, I have to share this. I look at him and know there is even more, much more. I am you, I am you, I AM YOU! Yes, yes, I see it. I am trembling with joy, I have always loved, always been, always will be, never alone, impossible, impossible, loved always and loving this way, without knowing, but knowing, always knowing.

"Do you feel it?" My voice is hushed, pleading. My eyes probe his beautiful face for hidden evidence of an experience he is for some inexplicable reason withholding from me. A pause ensues, his eyes meet mine and then scan the rain shelter for clues to my question. He looks puzzled and returns his gaze to my face. "Feel what?" he asks, soberly. Neither of us pursue the question, and seconds later he is back at the loom weaving his words. I look out at the trees beyond our enclosure and worship the spaces between the leaves, knowing what glue it is that binds these beings together, and how it is they sing.

*   *   *

Following the interview, Chris and I spent another hour and a half together talking. I did not want the afternoon to end. Later on, driving home with my husband, I struggled for words to describe my experience, and used the only ones I could. "Paul, I fell in love with a client today, do you think that's okay?" There was a long pause and my husband took his eyes off the road briefly to look at me. "I don't know," he said with a small edge in his voice. Neither did I.

Before I began to worry about the implications of my question, I believed this experience was the keystone, the essence of all healing. I knew from observation and personal history that this experience was the answer to our deepest need, and that it was capable of creating the most dramatic and positive, if not transformational, changes. When I shared my views with two or three professors, the comeback was always: "Yes, but is this the client's experience or is it yours?"

I had assumed it was mutual, but as I wrote the details of my wonderful encounter for the first time in my life, and prepared to go public with my perceptions, I could not escape a growing panic that I was the primary beneficiary of this experience, and by extension, of the counselling relationship itself. Was I doing something wrong? Did counselling really serve the client first and best? I was no longer sure, and began worrying about my clients' welfare, and my own motives for wanting to do this work. My training had taught me why such feelings for a client could be inappropriate or even dangerous: countertransference, projection, poor boundaries and professional ethics. Such an experience could cause me to victimize, or abuse, or confuse this individual with a friend, or–the ultimate desecration–a lover. I might, without meaning to, start leaning on the client emotionally. I might do anything, and the fact of my authority made that possibility an inescapable threat.

Conversely, the enormity of this experience made it impossible for me to doubt the simply fantastic knowledge, gratitude and impetus to service it embodies. In simple terms, the experience informs me beyond the shadow of a doubt that I love this client, personally, even intimately, and with a passion rarely felt even for those closest to me in my own life. Passion? Love? Do I not mean empathy? In its milder form perhaps. But this experience goes beyond the sense of deep empathic connection where I have a sense of confidence and ease, of being "touched" by the client and "in touch" with our process.

Lexicon has been a problem from the beginning. I did not know what to call this momentous experience, and am still not sure. For awhile I favored the term "Third Thing" because it evoked the sense of sacred presence that I have experienced when I am deeply engaged with another person, be it a stranger, family member, friend, lover, or client. However, my experience has many names, according it values ranging from the sinister to the sublime, from the esoteric to the everyday, from the pathological to the peak of human experience. Early in my research, after reading Stace's (1960) book on mysticism, my problem was solved when I found my experience described accurately and in detail as an "extrovertive mystical experience." I began to use the term "mystical" and was further encouraged to do so by the extensive and influential work of Ralph Hood (1974, 1975, 1976, 1977, 1979) who based his work, and developed a mysticism scale, on Stace's theory.

In the deepest moment of this experience, it is as if a window opens and allows me to glimpse, and *experience*, to my utter stupefaction and inexpressible joy, the simple truth and answer to my very existence: I am the Other and the Other is me. Not in any metaphorical sense, nor in any way that occludes my own sense as a separate self. I am myself *and* You in the same instant. Somehow I "know" this and the knowledge is obvious, absolute and stunning. Within it lies the treasure; the certainty that I am unfathomably loved, and that my greatest yearning and privilege are to serve this sacred being–this Other–who sits before me. The problem is that I do not know what to give, or how to give it. This "mystical" engagement beckons me to an act of devotion, of service, of commitment that falls outside my professional mandate. In the light of this experience my skill base, my training, the theories, and my professional role turn to ashes, and I am humbled to my core.

In my experience with Chris, no "therapeutic response" was in the realm of possible options to offer. All paled in comparison to the staggering beauty and integrity I perceived in him, and which enveloped us both. Anything I could do as a counsellor would simply diminish, and impose on, or corrupt, the perfection. At one point I remember scanning my mind in disbelief, finding there was nothing to be done, and coming to what seemed like more adequate, if unprofessional alternatives. Thus, I found myself wondering if I should offer Chris my sweater, or extend my hand to hold his, or get up from my seat to embrace him. Perhaps I could honor him with the gift of tears welling up behind my composed facade, or invite him home for some dinner. In the end, I did nothing but continue to listen until the story was finished. However, the seed of conflict between my professional knowledge and my personal experience was sown. Seeing this spark of divinity before me, embraced in the sacred shelter of this relationship, and knowing the depth of its meaning in my own life, I have a terrible decision to make: what can I do? What *must* I do for this person?

Through the process of writing an autobiographical study on this experience, and its impact on my work and my life, I have come to some conclusion, although I still do not know how to implement it within my work, or even if I can. The journey to this answer has been through the process of writing my own stories. Through them I explored and discovered the presence of this experience from earliest memory onwards. I became more familiar with the terror of sharing my ecstatic experience with others; this was a very private, not a public experience. The nature of my terror also revealed itself to be bound to the very oppression I experienced as a woman and a student, and that I struggled to avoid perpetuating as a counsellor. Through my stories I also confronted the taboo of loving clients, and my professional complicity in pathologizing the emotional fallout of culturally endorsed violence and denial. I acknowledged the bogey of sexuality within the context of counselling work, and the specter of client abuse. I also came to accept the wisdom of what Audre Lorde (1989) calls the "erotic." Finally, I recognized my inability to avoid the power imbalance inherent in the counselling paradigm, and my willingness to be paid three times for the work I do as a counsellor. That is, once for the relationship, once for the privileges of my position, and once in cash. Through this long process, this storying of my experience and knowledge, I came to the following conclusion.

My experience of mystical love is not just a state of ecstatic bliss, it is a call to action and justice. The issue of justice has brought the greatest clarity to the many conflicts and concerns that emerged in my study which I reduced to the two overriding issues I face as a counsellor. The concerns are of taking too much from the client, or of giving too much of myself away. Although my greatest discomfort has focused on the fear of taking too much–of abusing or harming the client in some way–it is the second concern that raises the most interesting questions for me as a counsellor. Fear of doing too much for the client tends to keep me defensive, passive, toothless, and safe. Safe from sticking my neck out, from speaking the truth, and from taking risks that might in some way harm my privilege, or my professional equanimity.

So what if I got overinvolved? What if I did love that client passionately and he or she knew it without hesitation? What if I overextended myself way beyond the boundaries of my professional protocol? The most succinct and validating answer I have found to date comes from the writing of Matthew Fox (1979) and Carter Heyward (1989), who articulate what I have already found through my own experience. Their answer is, simply enough: I would recognize that my love for Other, and my desire for justice, are the same thing. "Love which is not an acute sense of justice and an authentic suffering with my outraged brother (or sister), such love *does not transcend*" (Miranda, cited in Fox, 1979, p. 16). Fox tells me what I already know through my encounters with clients: that when I love the Other, I am involved in my greatest self-interest. Further, that my professional motivation can not be seen as altruistic, for this word supposes a separation between my client and I that does not exist. I need not fear my love for clients, these writers assure me, while reminding me of the enormous task it involves.

> To really love is to topple unjust structures, bringing down the principalities and powers of domination and control at all levels of human social relations. . . . To love you is to be pushed by a power/God both terrifying and comforting, to touch and be touched by you. To say "I love you" means–*let the revolution begin*! (Heyward, 1989, pp. 300-301)

It is from this vantage point that I have found the counselling paradigm so profoundly compromising, for unless I am actively involved in "the marvellous dismantling" (Heilbrun, 1988, p. 62) that will help me create justice for my client, how can I defend my work? This is no easy task, for I still do not know how to challenge my own privilege and justify it at the same time; that is the double bind. Whatever the work of justice means for my future as a counsellor, I am sure of one thing. I do not want to hide my passionate love for clients to assuage my own discomfort and safeguard my privilege. Neither do I want to deny it to keep myself insulated from the overwhelming task of confronting the oppression that keeps so many coming to our doors.

REFERENCES

Fox, M. (1979). *A spirituality named compassion and the global village, humpty dumpty and us.* Minneapolis: Winston Press.

Heilbrun, C. G. (1988). *Writing a woman's life.* New York: Ballantine.

Heyward C. (1989). Sexuality, love, and justice. In J. Plaskow & C. P. Christ (Eds.), *Weaving the visions: New patterns in feminist spirituality* (pp. 293-301). New York: HarperCollins.

Hood, R. W. (1979). Personality correlates of the report of mystical experiences. *Psychological Reports, 44,* 804-806.

Hood, R. W. (1977). Differential triggering of mystical experience as a function of self actualization. *Review of Religious Research, 18,* 264-270.

Hood, R. W. (1976). Mystical experience as related to present and anticipated future church participation. *Psychological Reports, 39,* 1127-1136.

Hood, R. W. (1975). The construction and preliminary validation of a measure of reported mystical experience. *Journal for the Scientific Study of Religion, 14,* 29-41.

Hood, R. W. (1974). Psychological strength and the report of intense religious experience. *Journal for the Scientific Study of Religion, 13,* 65-71.

Lorde, A. (1989). Uses of the erotic: The erotic as power. In J. Plaskow & C. P. Christ (Eds.), *Weaving the visions: New patterns in feminist spirituality* (pp. 208-213). New York: HarperCollins.

Stace, W. T. (1960). *Mysticism and philosophy.* London: Macmillan.

Exploring Intimacy in Therapy: Broadening the Interpretation of Arousal

RuthAnn Parvin

SUMMARY. Case material is used to explore the idea that ambiguous autonomic arousal may be "overtranslated" as sexual arousal, both by therapists and by clients. As a result, other important aspects of intimacy in relationships do not get taught or discussed in supervision/therapy. *[Article copies available for a fee from The Haworth Document Delivery Service: 1-800-342-9678. E-mail address: getinfo@haworth.com]*

Many years ago that seem like yesterday, I sat in a small therapy room with one of my first clients, a very young woman who reminded me of a doe on the edge of a forest clearing, aware and ready to bolt if her sense of danger increased the tiniest iota. It was a hard session. She was dealing with the pain of parental abuse and of gang rape by adolescent males with twisted ideas about masculinity and their duty to teach a young woman the meaning of being female. In her silence of searching for words to tell me about something that had never been put into the stark reality of language, and in the occasional silent tear that moved slowly down the contour of her face, I felt her vulnerability and shame. I remember that a shaft of late

---

This article was written by a clinical psychologist who has a hard time deciding whether she'd rather go to a dentist for a 24 hour drilling marathon or submit an article for critique. RuthAnn Parvin, JD, PhD, a clinical psychologist, is sole proprietor, Chief of Staff, and CEO of A Place to Talk Counseling Services.

Address correspondence to: RuthAnn Parvin, 2925 S.E. Taylor, Portland, OR 97214-4032.

[Haworth co-indexing entry note]: "Exploring Intimacy in Therapy: Broadening the Interpretation of Arousal." Parvin, RuthAnn. Co-published simultaneously in *Women & Therapy* (The Haworth Press, Inc.) Vol. 20, No. 1, 1997, pp. 69-71; and: *More than a Mirror: How Clients Influence Therapists' Lives* (ed: Marcia Hill) Harrington Park Press, an imprint of The Haworth Press, Inc., 1997, pp. 69-71. Single or multiple copies of this article are available for a fee from The Haworth Document Delivery Service [1-800-342-9678, 9:00 a.m. - 5:00 p.m. (EST). E-mail address: getinfo@haworth.com].

spring sunlight cut across the wall but we sat on the shaded side of the room. It was the first time I had experienced the shattering honor of another person trusting me to walk with her down the private but well-worn path of horrendous experience, towards a yearning for a life where trust and love could once again exist.

After the session, I realized that my body had responded in ways that, up until that time, I had only associated with sexual arousal. It frightened me. In my still simple understanding of therapy, sexual arousal toward a client was verboten–so forbidden that I could not even raise it with my supervisor for fear of being thrown out of my doctoral program.

However, as I thought about the session and about my countertransference, I realized that, despite the physical arousal, there had been no feeling of sexual desire during the session. I then began to wonder if the same signs of physiological arousal happened in non-sexual encounters. As a good graduate student, I started in the library and I read about the World War II Russian soldiers being treated for the pain of erections rubbing against their uniforms in the winter cold. Then I remembered a Viet Nam vet who had participated in some research with me, telling me late one night about his shame at having an erection during his first firefight. We both accepted that he must have been turned on by the violence. Now I began to wonder.

Finally, I began to talk with my classmates, very circumspectly and then with more confidence. "Yes," said one friend. "I get erections after I've toked a joint and I'm lying on the rug in the dark listening to my favorite jazz recordings." "Well I think so," said another who taught deaf pre-schoolers. "When I button the coat of one of the kids in my classroom and I think about the family situation she is returning to, I feel something deep inside of me contract–but it's not sexual. It's that I feel so sad for her." And finally, "Sweet Jesus, have you ever stepped off a curb and almost been hit by a truck coming around the corner? You better bet you cream yourself."

Gradually I came to know, within myself, that my experience was not that of being sexually turned on by my client or my client's pain and I was able to talk to my supervisor about what had happened. I shared with him my conclusion that physiological arousal, partially registered in the genital region, is a reaction to many strong emotions: danger, connection, love, vulnerability, and also, but not always, sexual desire. In one of the best supervision sessions I ever had, we discussed "countertransference" in terms of the gift of deep knowledge that comes from paying attention to our bodies, our intuitions, and our sense of connection (or lack of it) with our client. Countertransference was not pathologized but rather seen as another mode for gathering information and for growth–sometimes in the therapist, sometimes in the client.

This knowledge has helped me, through the years, connect as a therapist with men who have molested their children and those who did the opposite, physically and emotionally distancing themselves from their children when they experienced autonomic arousal looking at the child; with war veterans who have gotten erections during horrendous moments of inhumane behaviors towards the enemy; and with therapists who have broken the boundaries of appropriate behaviors towards their clients. Sometimes the quick sexual interpretation of our arousal prevents us from looking at the deeper yearning for and fear of connection with others that goes far beyond sexual intercourse.

I believe that these behaviors are often translation errors. Our body's arousal speaks an ambiguous language and, perhaps because of our culture, we tend to over-translate it into a sexual message and then either act it out inappropriately or inhibit it without learning from it. Or, out of embarrassment and fear of criticism, we avoid consulting when we need help exploring the meaning of our responses.

As I mature as a therapist, I feel such humility and gratitude for the awesome bright beauty of the human soul that is again and again revealed to me by my clients as they share the dark corners of their memories and deeds in their search for something shining and new. And I celebrate that my body, mind, and soul rise up and respond to this beauty.

The Wish to Become a Mother

Gloria Rose Koepping

SUMMARY. Therapists who treat pregnant women while trying to conceive themselves have a variety of emotional reactions. These countertransferential feelings are outlined and discussed from the view of one therapist attempting to become a mother herself. *[Article copies available for a fee from The Haworth Document Delivery Service: 1-800-342-9678. E-mail address: getinfo@haworth.com]*

I'm at that time in my life when I've become focused on my desire to have a child. After convincing myself that I have the emotional and psychological ability to do so, I've been actively trying to get pregnant for over a year. Currently, I've decided to take a few more months to use alternative insemination and then shift to saving money to adopt.

With this position as my backdrop, I sit and see pregnant college students every week. Many of the pregnant clients that I see have no work skills, will drop out, and have no money, job, health care, family support, or a partner. Some already have one or two children. Most of these clients did not use any birth control and would not consider adoption or abortion for religious or spiritual reasons.

Gloria Rose Koepping, PhD, is Coordinator of Psychological Services in the Counseling Center at Highline Community College, Des Moines, WA. At her college she works predominantly with economically and educationally disadvantaged women.

The author would like to thank Tracy Maynard for her editorial assistance.

Address correspondence to: Gloria Rose Koepping, Highline Community College, Counseling Center 6-10, 2400 South 240th Street, Des Moines, WA 98198 or e-mail (gkoeppin@hcc.ctc.edu).

[Haworth co-indexing entry note]: "The Wish to Become a Mother." Koepping, Gloria Rose. Co-published simultaneously in *Women & Therapy* (The Haworth Press, Inc.) Vol. 20, No. 1, 1997, pp. 73-76; and: *More than a Mirror: How Clients Influence Therapists' Lives* (ed: Marcia Hill) Harrington Park Press, an imprint of The Haworth Press, Inc., 1997, pp. 73-76. Single or multiple copies of this article are available for a fee from The Haworth Document Delivery Service [1-800-342-9678, 9:00 a.m. - 5:00 p.m. (EST). E-mail address: getinfo@haworth.com].

My countertransference issues with these clients spew forth as an unrelenting obsessive stream of angry, worrisome, and judgmental thoughts. I find myself vacillating between resentment and intense guilt about my judgmental feelings. I struggle with these feelings almost daily.

When I see a pregnant client I sometimes get angry, and my compassion and patience leave me. How come this person with no job, work skills, house, or partner gets to be pregnant and I don't? It's not fair. I'm ready now. Why not me? I waited until after I was through school–I did the smart thing. Or did I? Sometimes I sit and tell myself it wouldn't have been any good if I had tried before now because I wasn't ready; it wouldn't have happened. Waiting was the right thing to do. But my anger is not that easily placated.

I worry, too. I worry that I won't get pregnant. I worry that I will. But I want a child. I want to be a mother. All this is in my head, floating through my mind even as I ask my client how she is feeling this week. I remind her that she can leave and go to the bathroom if she needs to. I take care of her.

Doing therapy with pregnant clients while trying to conceive has made me more aware of my own judgmentalness as a therapist. It forces me to ask myself if I am really angry with them or my own life situation. Maybe I'm even angry at my clients' parents for not emotionally supporting them and their educational endeavors. I imagine that is why some clients of mine see that having a child is their only chance to be successful at something. Understanding the utility of my client's choices and behaviors allows me to be less judgmental and more helpful as a therapist.

I come from the same community and social class of people that I work with. This background results in my being more judgmental and less understanding than perhaps other therapists might be. I examine this phenomenon as a class and gender issue. I continue to work to sort out my own biases and reactions.

Clients remind me why I left and what messages I got from my community that weren't supportive. I forget sometimes and blame my clients for the worth that is placed on women and education in our area. Then I need to realign myself on my client's side and help her question whether all she can do with her life is mother. When I see a woman who appears lazy or unmotivated, I tell myself it's because she has been unsupported or belittled in her educational aspirations. I need to remember that every woman I work with has more potential than she thinks she has, even if she isn't academically strong. I can teach her how to work the system, use the skills she has and package herself in a way acceptable to employers or other schools. I remind myself never to assume my clients have the financial ability to avail themselves of extra educational opportunities that come along. I also need to acknowledge my clients' resourcefulness. Finally, I try not to compare myself with my clients. Although our life situations and influences may be overlapping, we also are very different in many ways. It is never a fair comparison. I can encourage and promote them, but never expect them to make the same life choices I did (or conversely, to expect myself to make the same choices they did).

Often I have to tell myself that no matter what has happened to these women or what happens to me, that my job right now is to help this particular woman with her choice. I struggle to remember to ask how her amniocentesis went, if she has enough maternity clothes, if she needs me to help her locate a crib, if her doctor is listening to her, if we need to consult her M.D. about an antidepressant yet or not. As a psychologist I was trained to assist my clients with pragmatic tasks; in addition to exploring their psychological issues, for example, asking about their plans for this child-to-be. I prompt the client to put together the nursery I wish I had. I care about each woman and her child. When she leaves my office, I wish even more that I was putting together my nursery, my crib, my shelves of cute little clothes.

I listened this week to a woman talk of her obstetrician, who didn't know how to handle her size, and what he needed to do to accommodate her during her amniocentesis. He didn't know how to have her hold her stomach up so he could get a better chance at locating her uterus. Since he wasn't familiar with the techniques for use with larger women, the procedure wasn't successful and had to be redone at another hospital. My client was humiliated and angry. She wondered if big women who are pregnant are scary for some people. I wonder if I will become scary to other people if I become pregnant.

In the past, I've helped pregnant women with histories of sexual abuse prepare for the pain of labor. I've had consultation conference calls with labor and delivery teams to help them prepare for a germ phobic obsessive-compulsive client. I've visited women in the hospital after their C-sections to support them and applaud their efforts. I've helped new mothers grieve the death and loss of a child as well as accept their children who have been born with birth defects and special needs. Sometimes I think I have the compassion I do because I value children so much. Because I want one so much.

This wish to be a mother has caused me so much disappointment that I've talked with some colleagues as well as my therapist. All are sympathetic but in different life situations than I am. The ones who want children have them. The ones who don't, don't have them. It seems they are content. I still long to have a child. If wishing could make it so, I'd be a mother now.

But I am not a mother. I wonder what is the lesson for me in this uncomfortable situation. What good can I find in it? In what directions can this experience lead me? I realize I can still be of tremendous help to women even if I don't share all of their life experiences (such as having birthed a child). Along the way I'm reminded that I learn from my client's insights too. I've also come to believe that I don't have to have every issue resolved in my life in order to be of assistance to someone else. I can hear some long-forgotten supervisors tell me that being comfortable with ambivalence is what makes a good therapist. I'm still working at that.

So here I sit wondering if I'll become pregnant, or adopt. What if I don't have a child? Will I be able to find a way to mother? Will I be generative or productive some other way? Will I be happy with what happens? I wish I knew how this will all turn out. What will be? I am impatient and anxious to find out.

Victims, Survivors, and Veterans: A Circle of Courage

M. Sue Crowley

SUMMARY. The article describes a self-help group experience with victim/survivors of sexual abuse. By highlighting one group member's story of incestuous abuse and paternal pimping, the facilitator examines how her own thoughts and feelings about sexual abuse evolved from a psychological perspective based on individual survival to a better understanding of political, group resistance. The need to develop further a language of resistance that highlights both women's political and personal courage is discussed. The term "veteran" is offered as an adjunct to the use of "victim/survivor" because it connotes both honor and courage, providing a defiantly proud term with which to identify sexually abused women. As an addition to the discourse on victimization, "veteran" implies a political awareness of women's age-old struggle against sexual oppression and honors those who openly challenge the status quo. *[Article copies available for a fee from The Haworth Document Delivery Service: 1-800-342-9678. E-mail address: getinfo@haworth.com]*

Every Tuesday morning through that winter, the group met in a windowless basement room of the women's shelter downtown. It was a small

M. Sue Crowley, PhD, is Assistant Professor of Human Development, School of Education and Human Development at Binghamton University. Her writing and research interests are focused on issues in feminist multicultural pedagogy and the impact of sexual abuse on women's development.

Address correspondence to: M. Sue Crowley, LT302, SEHD, Binghamton University, Binghamton, NY 13902 or (scrowley@bingsuns.edu).

[Haworth co-indexing entry note]: "Victims, Survivors, and Veterans: A Circle of Courage." Crowley, M. Sue. Co-published simultaneously in *Women & Therapy* (The Haworth Press, Inc.) Vol. 20, No. 1, 1997, pp. 77-81; and: *More than a Mirror: How Clients Influence Therapists' Lives* (ed: Marcia Hill) Harrington Park Press, an imprint of The Haworth Press, Inc., 1997, pp. 77-81. Single or multiple copies of this article are available for a fee from The Haworth Document Delivery Service [1-800-342-9678, 9:00 a.m. - 5:00 p.m. (EST). E-mail address: getinfo@haworth.com].

town in the hill country of central Pennsylvania where winters are often long and hard. Some women drove an hour or more to get there. Cramped and often cold, we usually began with a "check-in" around the circle that evolved into lengthy conversations, revelations, and confessions about our past and present lives.

At first, I approached the group with both confidence and curiosity. During a ten-year stint as a supervising therapist in a rural community mental health center, I had handled many crisis situations and facilitated other groups for women. Although I had never before worked with a group consisting exclusively of sex abuse victim/survivors, I viewed this experience as a welcome challenge. Yet, I was to discover that nothing I had done before, either as a feminist academic or an experienced therapist, rivaled the raw emotional power and thought-provoking intensity of those cramped meetings.

Our corner basement room was lit with harsh artificial light, seeming to reflect back at us some inexorable truth-in-circumstance. Hidden there in the relative safety of the underground, we could attempt to voice the truths of our lives, slowly overcoming the shame that has kept women silent and alone for centuries. Over time, I became aware of some unspoken emotion, something without a name, in the struggle to move beyond survival and to capture a sense of shared pride in our existence. One woman's tale became emblematic of that struggle.

I remember her story this way.[1]

I was small, very small, only about eight when it happened. It wasn't the first time. I was traveling with Him on one of his many business trips to a strange city (I was lucky, they said, to have a father who loved me so much that, even after the divorce, He would make such special time for me in His life). It was late. Locked in the bathroom of our hotel room, I huddled terrified and alone. Waiting . . . , listening. Sometimes, He came back alone. Other times, He brought men with him. He would watch, goad, enjoy, occasionally join in, but He always collected the money.

This night, I waited with a razor in my hand. Squeezed in a corner between the wall and the toilet, I strained to hear, was it one set of footsteps or two? I could survive His hands on me again, but not more, not the others. I wasn't sure how exactly, I was very small after all, but I knew I could . . . must. Straining to hear, one or two? One, I lived. Two, I died. The blade could slice so deep, so fast, not even He could stop it. Then, He would be left with no more than my small, bloody body. No more goods for sale.[2]

She told her story with a quiet pride, assuring us that the silence had given way to the sound of one set of footsteps in the night. Otherwise, she would not have been there to tell it. In that calm determination to die, she revealed the courage of a girlchild to take the one path of resistance left open to her, the only way to defeat the omniscience of His worldly power over her. I sat silent, awestruck by the images and torn with ambivalence. What victory was there in death? What courage in suicide? What Masada of a child's soul was this?

Masada. As she spoke, the word rose out of nowhere in my mind. And with it came a vague memory of the ancient legend of a place called Masada. The people were trapped within the walls of their fortress on a high plateau, surrounded by a massive enemy force that controlled their water and food supply. They must choose the slow death of thirst and starvation or, perhaps worse, surrender and be reduced to a fate less than life in foreign slavery. They killed their children first, then the women and men, until only one rabbi was left. He killed himself. Ever after, I thought of that terrified little girl with her desperate courage as a Masada child.

I remained troubled by the jumble of images and the powerful emotions they evoked in me. Something was missing. Not missing in the women of the group or their very different ways of surviving the hard truths of their lives, but in me. I needed a new way of understanding the choices each of us must make, often alone and with few, if any, good options. Drawn by the power of their telling voices, I began to see the women of our circle in a different light. In those instances when shame gave way to rage and anger flashed into a bitter pride in their own existence, I came to view our small circle as a place of great power.

Searching for some other language, some other words to describe the struggle, I began to think of incested and raped women as veterans in a war even more ancient than the legend of Masada. Each of the women in the group had resisted the claims of our patriarchal culture, fighting to regain a sense of self with honor. "Veteran" is a word of honor, often reserved for men who have served in peacetime or fought in wars. Co-opting these images of service and combat survival, I sought a word that would lend honor and pride to many different women and that would simultaneously undermine the pervasive social shaming of women who have been victim/survivors of sexual assault.

From my feminist and academic training, I was familiar with the discourse on "victimization," but these new perceptions came from a different place, from a visceral knowledge. That terrible image of a helpless, suicidal child became transformed into the symbol of a freedom fighter. No surrender. At first, I shied away from this image and the powerful feelings it evoked. The political intellectual in me was afraid of thinking in some linear hierarchy of recovery: victim to survivor to veteran. We have enough trouble dealing with our differences without adding more dividing lines. Yet, as the women in the group voiced their own misgivings about what to call themselves, victims or survivors, indicating their dissatisfaction with both, I became more convinced that we need a consciously, defiantly proud language of identity for sexually abused women.

As we know too well, the struggle to escape victimization cannot always be won. Not all victims are survivors. Some suffer the anonymous martyrdom of a child suicide, while others remain lost in alcohol or other drugs, self-destructive lives that are a reflection of the social shame so many rape and incest victims endure. And not all survivors would want to identify themselves as "veterans." Some choose a personal rather than political meaning for their experience, preferring to envision themselves as individuals who continue to overcome the personal tragedies of their lives. But others seek to lend a different meaning to their personal tragedies by seeing them as part of larger social struggle. They are veterans: women who reclaim their lives in defiance of the social shaming of sex abuse victims, emboldened by the awareness of their group status as descendants of an ancient and honorable line of women warriors.

There is no shame in being a "victim," but the term does imply an ongoing state of helplessness. "Survivor," in turn, suggests that raped and incested women experienced a tragic accident of fate, rather than a deliberate outrage with deep social, as well as personal, meanings. Assuming a group identity, "veterans" are situated within the complex matrix of a personal-social-political sphere.[3] This matrix includes several dimensions of experience, including one's individual victimization and survival, as well as a sociopolitical awareness of sexual assault as a weapon used to enforce a patriarchal status quo. Unlike survivors, sex abuse veterans act openly in defiance of that status quo, unwilling to remain hidden in self-help groups or alone in therapy.

Far from offering a hierarchy of recovery, however, the group helped me to become aware of the extent to which women combine many positions and perspectives. Sometimes, we are victims. Sometimes, we can only hope to survive until things get better. Other times, we come out from underground to challenge the status quo. It is in making that challenge, in acting out our resistance, that victim/survivors lay claim to the status of veterans. We wait in the relative safety of our hidden groups, but we must also stand up to take back the night.

By the end of that long winter, I had accepted a job in another state and prepared to say goodbye to the group. At our last meeting I didn't know how to explain my gratitude for the gift they had given me. Realistically, I believed that rape could never be stopped. In the face of such inexorable injustice, a sense of helpless outrage often left me with no focus for my anger. The turning point came about midway through the winter, while bearing witness to that small girlchild huddled in a corner by a toilet, waiting to die. It was then, the darkest time of year, I began to see that among us in the circle were the scarred, but proud "veterans" of an ancient battle. A confusion of tears came to me then, tears for many emotions, both good and bad, and for many often helpless, but no less brave women, both here and gone. I emerged from underground no longer exhausted by helpless rage, but fueled with the anger of action. That was their gift to me.

Yet, their images and stories have continued to haunt me. Time and again, I think of those women huddled in that basement bunker and wonder: What do we, the "facilitators," enmeshed in the individualistic language of therapy and the practice of "self"-help, have to offer those for whom personal survival is not enough? And where is that hidden army of shameless women, waiting to claim their honored status as veterans? We need to add a third dimension to the language of recovery from sexual assault, a deliberately defiant language, if we are to provide more than the cold comfort of basement bunkers. When survival is not enough, resistance is necessary.

I will end with news of the now grown veteran of the story told above. In our second phone conversation about this paper, she told me she intends to create a ritual in which she awards herself medals for courage. She also hopes to incorporate the idea of a medal ceremony in her next Take Back the Night march.

ENDNOTES

1. The woman whose story is recounted here was the first to read and review the manuscript. She has given me her permission to include this account of the incident.

2. The use of capital letters to designate the male pronoun that identifies the abuser in this story is deliberate. It is employed as a means of indicating his power over the child, both in terms of its patriarchal reality and as it must have been perceived by the child.

3. It would be six months before I read Judith Herman's groundbreaking work, *Trauma and Recovery* (1992), in which she makes explicit the links between war veterans and abused women. I remain indebted to her and others, especially incest veterans themselves, for further insights into the complex matrix of personal-social-political dynamics that describe their lives.

Border-Crossing on a Racist Terrain

Nayyar S. Javed

SUMMARY. Being a racialized woman and doing therapy with mostly white clients creates an intersection of race and gender that affects the role I am supposed to perform as a helper. The intersection of race and gender causes transference and countertransference that need to be resolved in therapy. The interplay of transference and countertransference is conceptualized as a border-crossing in this article.

Most of my clients have helped me in gaining awareness of my struggle of border-crossing. However, two of my clients seemed to have a greater impact in this regard. A white, male client openly admitted the transference he was experiencing because of my cultural origin. A racialized woman's struggle of border-crossing in terms of seeking justice as a Canadian citizen revealed how justice was denied to her because of her racial and cultural origins and how a counsellor justified it by blaming the culture of my client. *[Article copies available for a fee from The Haworth Document Delivery Service: 1-800-342-9678. E-mail address: getinfo@haworth.com]*

Being a non-white woman and doing therapy with mostly white clients is a transgression of boundaries that divide people on what Dubois (1992)

Nayyar S. Javed, MEd (United States), MEd (Canada), is a feminist therapist at the Saskatoon Mental Health Clinic in Saskatoon, Saskatchewan.

Address correspondence to: Nayyar S. Javed, Saskatoon Mental Health Clinic, 4th Floor Birks Building, 165-3rd Avenue South, Saskatoon, SK, S7K 1L8, Canada.

[Haworth co-indexing entry note]: "Border-Crossing on a Racist Terrain." Javed, Nayyar S. Co-published simultaneously in *Women & Therapy* (The Haworth Press, Inc.) Vol. 20, No. 1, 1997, pp. 83-90; *More than a Mirror: How Clients Influence Therapists' Lives* (ed: Marcia Hill) Harrington Park Press, an imprint of The Haworth Press, Inc., 1997, pp. 83-90. Single or multiple copies of this article are available for a fee from The Haworth Document Delivery Service [1-800-342-9678, 9:00 a.m. - 5:00 p.m. (EST). E-mail address: getinfo@haworth.com].

83

calls "Color-line." This demarcation of the boundaries determines who should or should not be a helper.

Historically, the professional paid helper has often been a white, middle-class heterosexual man. The representation of this man is contrasted with the rest of the population by constructing all "others" as essentially lacking the ingredients deemed necessary for this kind of helping. This deficit is portrayed as biological and cultural, and often culture and biology are intermixed and seen as one entity.

In the past, assuming biological deficits within various populations, including women and the racialized groups, has served as a tool for constructing otherness, which has been used to disenfranchise these groups. In the current discourse on diversity, cultural "difference," which is often translated as "deficit," has gained prominence.

A lucrative business has emerged in the mental health field. Suddenly, professionals who have no critique of racism have become experts on fixing racial inequities by increasing cross-cultural understanding. The end result is the creation of "culturally different" as an entity that has few commonalities with the dominant group. The boundaries that set apart the "culturally different" are drawn on color lines but are represented as a natural concomitant of cross-cultural difference. Somehow, cultural difference is seen as so ingrained within individuals that nothing can erase it. Thus, essentializing "cultural difference" legitimates those boundaries that separate the entitled and disenfranchised, helper/helpee and good and bad. Moral arguments are enmeshed with scientific explanations of the difference. This enmeshment has existed since the inception of colonization. The legitimacy granted to colonization arises out of this enmeshment. It conceals the piracy of resources of the developing world by the West and exploitation of the racialized[1] within the Western countries.

The separation of "others" from the dominant group and race-based role division in the Western world forces someone like myself, who dares this role-reversal, to pay a price. As a therapist who is doing therapy with white clients, I transgress the boundaries that separate helper from the helpee.

I feel threatened from within on account of the internalization of the colonial imagery of the racialized peoples. This imagery constantly reminds me of the consequence of walking on a forbidden territory. This reminder engenders a deep sense of myself being an imposter. The self-doubt caused by seeing me as the imposter triggers the colonial images I am familiar with since my childhood.

---

1. I use the word "racialized" to reflect the social construction of racism.

I grew up in Pakistan in the post-independence years. Despite a strong sense of nationalism in people, they often expressed an awe for their colonizers and portrayed them as the "best" of the human species. Moving to Canada and experiencing marginalization may have deepened the images of the "best." After all, they are the privileged ones. I often ask myself, "What am I doing to erase these images?" and find it a struggle. Conceptualizing this struggle as countertransference arising out of the history of colonization has helped me in gaining an understanding of the dynamics within me and their interaction with what goes on within my clients.

Many of my white clients have been a wonderful resource in this regard. As well, many of my racialized clients have been helpful in assessing the impact of racism on people's lives and psychological makeup. In general, many of my clients have given me the gifts I need for doing effective therapy. However, I feel the need to acknowledge my appreciation for Adam and Ven who greatly enhanced my capacity for empathetic understanding of the border-crossing my clients have to go through in therapy as well as in their life struggles.

Ven, her husband and three small children left Vietnam in a small boat and were given refugee status in Canada in 1982. They came to live in Saskatoon. She, though a nurse from her own country of origin, started to work with a cleaning company. Her husband fell down in 1988 at his workplace and hurt his back. At that time, Ven came to see me. Her husband was unemployed, and their children were going through school; the eldest daughter Lee did well in high school and was accepted into university. Lee seemed to be doing very well in her studies but attempted suicide (by overdose). The family took turns being with her in the hospital. On the third day, the family had gone home to take care of a break-in; this was the only time they left her, assuming the hospital to be a safe place. However, Lee managed to go to another floor and hung herself with an electric cord in a washroom. Ven and her husband had many questions including why Lee was not seen, even once, by a psychiatrist and why the nursing staff left her unattended. The hospital administration refused to respond. Ven was asked to go through a lawyer. She did; he charged her ten thousand dollars in two years and did little. He wanted another five thousand dollars to pursue the case further. Ven could not afford to pay this amount and dropped the charges.

In order to deal with her daughter's suicide, Ven reached out to mental health services in the hospital and wanted to participate in a group for the families of suicide victims. The counsellor told her to seek help elsewhere because of Ven's limited English language skills. I went to talk to this counsellor in the hope of getting assistance for finding answers to Ven's questions.

I got nowhere with this counsellor. She silenced me by telling me that Lee's suicide was an inevitable outcome of her "shame-based culture." I should not have been shocked but I was. The knowledge of this counsellor's reputation as an expert on "grief" added to the sense of bewilderment I experienced at that moment. She was covering up a malpractice by blaming Lee's culture (in Saskatchewan all patients admitted for suicide attempts are required to see a psychiatrist, and Lee was not seen by one). According to the Saskatoon Mental Health legislation, Lee needed to be monitored, yet as soon as her family left the hospital, she was able to run to another floor, find an electric cord and hang herself. It must have taken time. Ven was asking, "Where was the hospital staff at that time?" and, "Why did they not notice Lee's absence from her bed?"

Ven had come to Canada as a refugee and had gone through several traumatic incidences, including witnessing death and destruction. Lee's suicide was one more blow, and the way this suicide was handled was yet another trauma. The series of traumas in her life made me more aware of the endless victimization refugee women endure during the chaotic situations they face to dislocate and also during the settlement process in a racially embedded society like Canada. I also realized that in the absence of a will to interrogate social and personal racism, no amount of training can help therapists to work effectively with the racialized population. The explanation of Lee's suicide, based on the characterization of her culture as "shame-based," pointed out ideological assumptions that can be brutal in therapy.

I do not deny the existence of shame in Lee's life and also in her suicide. But, her shame may have multiple sources, including the representations and treatment of "cultural difference." There seems to be little escape from these representations. They can destabilize the sense of self that evolves in a social context which never fails to reinforce the shame of being different than those whose privilege is guaranteed by their skin color, gender, class and sexual orientation. The "learned" counsellor seemed to have no consciousness about the two different social locations occupied by the privileged and underprivileged. She could not comprehend the self-hatred which can be engendered by those whose entrance to the space which would grant entitlement to its occupant is barred by many powerful forces. When border-crossing is prohibited, many of us turn inward in search of finding the causes of this prohibition, as if it were our fault. In my opinion, it is a natural consequence of oppression. Looking inward can cause shame, but may give us a false hope of opening those borders. We tend to delude ourselves by believing that if we can get rid of the "deficit" within us, we can lift the bars that stop border-crossing.

In order to take some proactive steps to prevent brutalities in therapy, the educational institutions preparing mental health professionals need to do some work. Understanding the impact of racism, sexism and other oppressive ideologies on people's lives is critical in this regard. But our educational institutions are part of a system that has no desire to make changes. The absence of courses in these areas and zero attempts at consciousness-raising in these institutions, therefore, are acts of compliance and collaboration in the perpetuation of oppression. In recent years, an occasional three hours or less seminar on "cross-cultural difference" is the only training offered in these institutions. It is a blatant refusal to acknowledge racism and other ideological forces that cause oppression.

I am quite aware of this refusal, yet faulting the educational institution did not prevent me from seeing this compliance and collaboration of the counsellor in Lee's case. Her allegiance to the "white system" made her participate in its atrocity against Ven. Her counsellor participated in silencing Ven by using her credentials and position of authority. She also attempted to silence me. When I asked her about giving some thought to the "shame" racialization can inflict on people like Lee, the counsellor continued her rhetoric about a shame-based culture.

Looking back at Ven's story, I realize that both Ven and myself, like millions of oppressed people, are locked in a space that takes away the legitimacy of our voice. But we delude ourselves about reclaiming our voice by border-crossing. We both have faith in our actions for transforming the system that neglected Lee's tragic death and silenced Ven.

I frequently interact with the counsellor who diagnosed people's oppression as an "outcome of" shame-based cultures. I seem to pretend that I have reconciled with her arrogance in making that diagnosis. This reconciliation by both Ven and myself reminds me of the slavery in the USA and subjugation of people all across the globe. The painful images of the slaves and other subjugated people struggling to border-cross, but who end up reconciled with their destiny, do remind me of the injustice that must be eradicated from the society and its institutions, including Mental Health.

In recent years, multiculturalism, which has accomplished nothing more than a few token changes, has given false hope to the racialized population in Canada. It has lured this population to accept racialized representations in the hope that understanding "cultural difference" will lead to equality. Consequently, a lucrative business has emerged for training people to understand this difference. But the consciousness of the cultural difference seems to increase rather than decrease the discord in the

Canadian population, a discord that was supposed to be eradicated by fostering inter-cultural understanding. In my case, these representations of the "culturally different" have implications for me as a racialized therapist.

Adam, a thirty-four-year old, white, heterosexual man, who had separated from his wife, contacted the clinic I work in for help. His two young children were living with their mother, and he was depressed and lonely. He was assigned to me. I called him and set up an appointment with him. Adam appeared anxious in our first encounter but opened up and talked about his recent pain and past history. Adam's father was an extremely cruel man who abused him and his mother. She died when Adam was nine, and his father married a woman with three children. The step-mother was extremely cruel to Adam, and she abused him in many ways. He was raped at age eleven by a neighbor. Adam had kept the secret, as he knew the consequences of revealing it—he knew no one would believe him, and he would be blamed for bringing it upon himself. Our subsequent sessions went very well. In the fourth session, Adam asked me if he could share something. I was curious and invited him to do so. He narrated some negative experiences with a few people of East-Indian origin and acknowledged that he did not think very highly of them. Therefore, he said, "When I found out that a 'Pakie' therapist would see me, I cursed my bad luck." Adam believed himself to be unlucky and "bad luck followed him" when he reached out for help.

Adam's honesty impressed me. I value his acknowledgement of what he thought of me. We discussed the role of representations of the "culturally-different" in our society in shaping people's consciousness. Adam was quite receptive and made some valuable connections between his life experiences and social representation of men. He continued contacting me even after the termination of therapy.

Adam opened the doors of his inner world and let me in, and it was an act of generosity. He enabled me to grasp the struggle of border-crossing my clients have to endure. Some hint at it but resolve its pull-push tensions, while others contact the clinic and ask for a different therapist. One of my clients who was a nurse but had aspirations of becoming a physician, interpreted my attempt to explore the impact of unfulfilled dreams as "cultural-difference." She believed that nursing is not valued in Pakistan (the country of my origin), and that was why I was probing the issue. She shared this interpretation with me and told me that it was her husband's opinion and so she would not see me. Her honesty was admirable, but she did not allow me to engage in a discussion that would have liberated her from the ideology which has separated the "culturally different" from others. She would have discovered her own anguish for giving up her struggle for border-crossing by giving up her aspirations.

Adam went through the classic dilemma of resisting and desiring border-crossing and switching helper/helpee roles. His initial reaction to seeing me was an act of resisting to move over, but his desire to dare transgression kept him engaged in therapy. Sharing this dilemma with me ultimately helped in its resolution. My other client did not allow herself to go through the push and pull inherent in this dilemma. Interpreting my exploring of her unfulfilled aspirations as only my "cultural difference" ended her work in resolving her dilemma.

I often find myself struggling with the same dynamic. It is tempting to resist the bonds that lock me in a restrictive space, but it is frightening to do so. The seduction to border-cross, and fear of the move, get played out in therapeutic contacts. Awareness of this interplay and its strategic use in therapy can be helpful in grasping other struggles of border-crossing into prohibited social spaces. For example, women who have been labelled with diagnostic categories but dare to resist this imposition, are engaged in these struggles. Understanding these struggles is an act of liberation from oppressive ideologies that alienate people from each other and from their authentic selves.

Like all acts of liberation, this act meets social reprisal which can be a blatant blow or an insidious mind game. The recently emerged discourse on "cultural difference" seems to fit in the latter category. It does a marvelous job in concealing racial inequities by representing the "culturally different" as unfit to be a "real Canadian," and therefore, the citizenship of such people becomes a "problematic issue." Their racialized allegiance to Canada is questioned because they ask for respect for their cultural identity. This perceived lack of allegiance to Canada legitimates racial inequities and also reinforces the notion that "culturally different" is permanently fixed. Cultures which give static, barbaric and pathological attributions to "different cultures" provide a contrast to the imagined racist-free, Canadian culture, a fiction that nobody knows and, therefore, has many versions. This contrast between the "Canadian" and "Other" cultures within Canada can have horrendous implications in therapy.

In my practice, I have met many "culturally different" individuals who are the casualty of this contrast. However, Ven, the refugee woman whose daughter committed suicide in a local hospital that handled the situation with zero compassion, impacted me differently. I was outraged. Being a mother, and also a racialized woman, I have witnessed many humiliating events that my son has gone through because of his skin color. Ven's tragedy brought all these issues to the surface. As an activist in the anti-racism movement, I felt challenged by this tragedy. As a therapist, I felt ashamed of belonging to the community of helping professionals. There was a mixture of overwhelming emotions that arose out of many parts of my own identity. I realized how difficult it was for me to separate myself from Ven. I wonder if I needed to separate despite my awareness of the boundary issues.

These images are a reminder of the salience of what Dubois (1992) calls "two-ness or an unreconciled striving within oneself" (p. 12) in doing therapy with the racialized and other subjugated populations. The seduction of the hope to change life by changing oneself and the fear of border-crossing engenders an inner division that causes alienation from the authentic self. The tension within reflects the duality in the society that divides people on "color-lines" but keeps inventing illusions that delude people to believe that their problems are caused by the lack of certain abilities.

As an activist, I often get invited for talk shows and public speaking, and invariably I come across people who are now using the concept of "cultural difference" as a source of racism. Multiculturalism gets blamed for "shoving strange cultures down people's throats." The argument made in this regard is that forcing people to accept other cultures has caused people to react in a racist way.

The illusions created by multiculturalism delude the dominant group as well as racialized Canadians. The former feels threatened while the racialized Canadians celebrate what they think is the end of their disenfranchisement. This celebration ends with experiences like the one endured by Ven.

Adam, in his honest and gentle way, made me realize the contempt I face in my struggle to border-cross as a response to the illusion created by multiculturalism. Ven reinforced my awareness of the consequences awaiting the racialized in border-crossing. I am thankful to both for coming into my life and shedding light on the spots hidden behind "cultural-difference" and multiculturalism on the racist terrain I have to travel on for the rest of my life.

REFERENCES

Dubois, W.E.B. (1992). *The souls of black folks.* Vintage Books/The Library of America.

hooks, b. (1994). *Outlaw culture: Resisting representations.* New York: Routledge.

Merger and Unconditional Love as Transformative Experiences

Rascha Levinson

SUMMARY. The author discusses experiences of merger and unconditional love she has had with different clients. These transcendent states have changed her practice and enlarged her personal life. *[Article copies available for a fee from The Haworth Document Delivery Service: 1-800-342-9678. E-mail address: getinfo@haworth.com]*

Merilee was a dark-haired, 36-year-old woman who came to therapy because her husband was addicted to heroin and she resented dealing with him. She told me how she and Steven lied to each other, manipulated and abused each other (she physically abused him, while he verbally abused her). They lived rent-free in an apartment building that her grandfather owned. Merilee had a profession, but she wanted to stay home and "do nothing." She was addicted to the Home Shopping Channel, and would buy things to have packages sent to her. This would relieve the emptiness she felt and was also a way of getting back at her parents, because they

---

Rascha Levinson, CSW, has been in private practice as a feminist therapist in New York City and Westchester for 25 years. She has been a member of, and held various offices in, AWP, FTI, AHP and NYSCSWP. She has one daughter and two grandsons. In the last fifteen years she has given papers and workshops at the New School in New York City and at national feminist conferences in the areas of relationships and creativity.

Address correspondence to: Rascha Levinson, 75 Sunset Drive, Ossining, NY 10562.

[Haworth co-indexing entry note]: "Merger and Unconditional Love as Transformative Experiences." Levinson, Rascha. Co-published simultaneously in *Women & Therapy* (The Haworth Press, Inc.) Vol. 20, No. 1, 1997, pp. 91-96; and: *More than a Mirror: How Clients Influence Therapists' Lives* (ed: Marcia Hill) Harrington Park Press, an imprint of The Haworth Press, Inc., 1997, pp. 91-96. Single or multiple copies of this article are available for a fee from The Haworth Document Delivery Service [1-800-342-9678, 9:00 a.m. - 5:00 p.m. (EST). E-mail address: getinfo@haworth.com].

paid all her charge card bills. Merilee wanted revenge against her husband, her parents, her brother, and the world for her unhappiness.

I disliked her from the first session. She had a whiny voice and the implication that other people should be making her happy was very clear. I think I felt threatened by her open avowal of feelings that I was afraid I might have myself. For instance, I felt contempt for her desire for revenge, which she stated very clearly and resentfully. I disliked her feelings of entitlement, allowing her family to pay for all sorts of things though she was (at least chronologically) a grown-up. I disliked her manipulations and lies, which had a strong revenge component.

I spent much time thinking about how to work with Merilee; I knew I had to change my attitude in order to work with her. I would wake up in the early morning, thinking about what I could say to her, what interpretations I could make that would give her some insight and help her to change. I set up an appointment to see her mother and father, hoping that would help me to understand her better. Her mother came alone—father was too busy to come, she said. Merilee's mother was a 50-year-old redhead, dressed in a tight pink skirt and a pink angora sweater, pink backless high-heeled shoes with gold trim.

Within the first five minutes she told me that she had been Miss Brooklyn when she was 17. Merilee's mother was clearly very self-involved and father was probably distant but supplied the money.

That evening I again thought of how I could help Merilee. I wasn't able to arrive at any definite ideas, and I finally went to sleep feeling exhausted. I remember thinking as I drifted into sleep "I just can't think about Merilee anymore—I give up."

The next time I saw Merilee, about five minutes after the beginning of the session I suddenly felt as if I were inside her body, looking out of her eyes and feeling her feelings. All her attitudes made sense to me. I felt her pain, her anger and frustration. This lasted throughout the session and for several sessions afterwards. It gradually faded, but after that I had no trouble with her attitudes and the therapy went well.

How did that happen? Just before I started working with Merilee, I had two clients who were very difficult for me, but even though I felt empathic towards them, I didn't dislike them the way I did Merilee. They both departed in unplanned terminations, which left me feeling frustrated and unhappy with my work. I tried very hard to figure out how to work with them but hadn't been able to. With Merilee, when I let go, I had this intense experience which felt transcendent, and which made this therapy much more successful than the other two. There seems to be a partial connection to the model of the creative process first constructed by Graham Wallas in 1926 (Harman and Rheingold, 1984). Wallas postulated that first there is a period of preparation–studying, researching, trying to solve the problem. Then comes a period of incubation, when the mind goes "off line," having given up. After this, usually at an odd time, comes illumination, the answer to the problem.

Another aspect of this experience with Merilee was described by M. Scott Peck (1978):

> An essential part of true listening is the discipline of bracketing, the temporary giving up or setting aside of one's own prejudices, frames of reference and desires so as to experience as far as possible the speaker's world from the inside, stepping inside his or her shoes.

This is probably the best linear way of describing my experience with Merilee. However, it has none of the startling emotional, transcendent feelings that I had with her. Over time, I had this same experience with some of my other clients, and it always came unexpectedly. I tried to learn to control this feeling so that I could have it at will. I tried putting myself in a trance, researching mystical experiences, going to various workshops and groups on intuition and altered states of consciousness. But none of this seemed to do it. And then I started to work with Dorsey.

In her first session, Dorsey told me a horrendous story of divorce, alcohol abuse, and the emotional absence of her family members, all as if she were making conversation at a tea party. At the end of the session I felt as if my brains were scrambled from the discrepancy between her tone and the content of what she told me. I also had a tremendous headache. As Dorsey talked in the next few sessions, it became clear to me that both father and mother rarely expressed any physical or verbal affection to her.

In the sixth session, D. talked about what it was like for her, at nine, when her parents divorced. She spent her after-school time alone in the apartment she shared with her mother (her brother lived with the father and her mother worked). I realized she was speaking with much more feeling than she had in the first session. Suddenly she was crying, in touch with the pain of that time. As I listened, I was flooded with love for Dorsey. Whatever she said or did, nothing would change that. I had no need to say anything about this to her, nor did I need her to love me back. It was enough simply to feel the love and total acceptance. It was a stunning and mysterious experience.

After this first experience, I found that I could feel this kind of unconditional love for some of my clients. This state, like my experience with Merilee and others, wasn't under my control. I could have it with some clients, but not with others. I believe that by opening themselves to me, my clients have given me the space to open myself to them, and in that opening is unconditional love.

I find that this is a very difficult experience to talk about–words simply don't express the feeling. I believe these experiences are not in my control. I can't make them happen. I think I can do certain things that encourage them to happen but there's no certainty that if I do these things, I will have this experience.

Articles in professional journals are generally written in a cognitive format, but this kind of experience doesn't fit into that form. It's like trying to explain a non-linear event in linear terms. In my experience with Merilee, it seemed to me as if for a while, I left my self, my body, and was able to look directly through her eyes and see the world as she did. That momentary experience affected me so strongly that my own viewpoint, my own values moved out of a central place, and after that I didn't have any difficulty with her point of view, or her feelings, and I stopped disliking her.

When I started working with Dorsey, I had no dislike for her; I felt sympathetic. The most intense part of my experience with her lasted about ten minutes, but the feelings lasted, in a quieter form, for the rest of our work together. My feelings of self seemed to be gone, and my boundaries expanded, so that I felt larger than usual. This was different than my sense of caring about a client. Caring about clients has a much more cognitive quality for me–it's a feeling, but the feeling is subtext to the understanding that clients are this way, I accept them because of their difficult childhood experiences. The feeling I had with Dorsey was different–it was like a Turner sky, or the Monet Waterlilies, all light and expansiveness, no sharp lines and suffused with love.

There were things I did that I believe encouraged these experiences. For example, I did quite a bit of research into quantum physics, which sees the world as a "soup" of energy, where all things are connected, different from Newton's world, which is made up of separate objects. This may have influenced my ability to see people and things as more connected. I attended many five-day workshops at growth centers like Esalen and Omega where no matter what the topic, one of the main learnings was that although we all have different personalities, on a deeper level we are all the same. In these workshops many people, myself included, felt one with others. I did a lot of Focusing (a meditative and body centered form of therapy) for a few years, with a very intuitive therapist, discovering that I am an intuitive person, which I had not known or even wondered about. I got interested in right brain phenomena and took a course in drawing with the right side of the brain. I had never been able to draw but in this course

I learned to draw by seeing in a new way, by focusing intently on line and mass and shape, ignoring any cognitive assessment that this was a person I was looking at.

I did these things for myself, without any thought for my clients, but at this point I think they also helped me as a therapist. I began to pay very, very close attention to all the details of my client's experiences. I would try to focus on them, on what they were saying, in the same way I had looked at the model in my drawing class. I realized that many times when I thought I had understood what my client was saying, I later found out that I had not really understood. This also led me to ask questions that often seemed to my clients to be dumb. She/he would look at me and say "But I just told you that!" in a tone that showed clearly how dense they thought I was. But I found that paying very close attention, eliciting the details of the experience–"and then what did she say?"–frequently led to the answers I was looking for. And this very close attention to detail seemed to bring me closer to an altered state of consciousness that has something to do with love.

I am able to feel this unconditional love for some clients but not for others. At this point, the clients I can feel love for are those who open more easily to me, or clients that I don't like, like Merilee. Clients that I have trouble with are those who are extremely, continually angry. I have difficulty with parents in therapy who have what I consider to be harmful beliefs, and discipline their children in hurtful ways. I think these are areas that I have to work on in myself. Clients' anger elicits my anger. I'm very sensitive to what I consider the mistreatment of children. However, even with these clients I am sometimes able to love them in this unconditional way–for a session here and there, or for parts of sessions. I believe that being able to feel unconditional love has improved the way I do therapy. Also, I feel wonderful when I experience giving this kind of love.

I think these experiences have helped me personally, have made me more aware of another dimension within myself. If my center of gravity was in a space four feet wide, a feeling-thinking-practical-person space, then through these experiences, one side of that space has opened up and expanded about two more feet to include another dimension, which could be called peak, transcendent, or spiritual. My center of gravity has shifted into the middle of this new space (that is, when I am centered!).

This shift has enabled me to have similar experiences even when I'm not doing therapy: I was walking through an arcade in Grand Central Station and there was a quartet playing the Pachebel Canon. I suddenly heard the music in a different way, as if I were lifted into a space where the notes were golden and glowing, and I could see/hear/feel them all at once.

Another time, in the autumn, I was walking near my house and ahead of me, on my right, I saw a stand of silver birches in a background of bare trees. The leaves on the birches were gold against the dappled white and black of the trunks. Again, suddenly, I seemed to lift out and up to another space and experienced for the first time knowing with absolute certainty in my gut that the trees are born as seedlings and grow through the spring, the summer, the fall and the winter, over and over again, the eternal round. And so do we humans. And when we die, the round goes on and we become part of that. I often see in the smile of a small child the same untrammeled joy I feel when I am having one of these experiences. They tap into a part of ourselves that we are not encouraged to be in touch with, living in such an extremely verbal, linear, left-brained and individualistic culture.

In writing this article, I have realized that maybe having had these experiences with my clients and seeing how this has helped me as a therapist, I trust that part of myself more; and I am more receptive to other kinds of experience coming from the same place in myself. This brings much joy into my life.

REFERENCES

Harman, W., & Rheingold, H. (1984). *Higher creativity: Liberating the unconscious for breakthrough insights.* Los Angeles: Jeremy Tarcher, Inc.

Peck, M. S. (1978). *The road less traveled.* New York: Simon & Schuster.

Female Therapist, Male Client:
Challenging Beliefs—
A Personal Journey

Beverley Kort

SUMMARY. This article explores the impact of gender on the relationship between female therapists and male clients. Integrating feminist and narrative ideas, the author relates some of her personal experiences in making gender issues more explicit in therapy. *[Article copies available for a fee from The Haworth Document Delivery Service: 1-800-342-9678. E-mail address: getinfo@haworth.com]*

My challenge and change has been in my work with men. I had always felt somewhat constrained with my male clients and did not like the impact it had on our therapy. I had talked to other women therapists about my difficulties and found that they had similar experiences. My problems became most evident to me when issues around privilege, gender and power needed to be discussed. I found myself caught between being too adversarial and challenging on the one hand and the "all giving" protector trained to soothe pain on the other. Here I was wanting to free my therapy from the constrictions of gender only to discover I was colluding to maintain them because I couldn't approach the subject without a sense of

Beverley Kort, MA, is a registered psychologist in private practice, Vancouver, British Columbia.

Address correspondence to: Beverley Kort, MA, #201-2245 W. Broadway, Vancouver, B.C. V6K 2E4, Canada.

[Haworth co-indexing entry note]: "Female Therapist, Male Client: Challenging Beliefs–A Personal Journey." Kort, Beverley. Co-published simultaneously in *Women & Therapy* (The Haworth Press, Inc.) Vol. 20, No. 1, 1997, pp. 97-100; and: *More than a Mirror: How Clients Influence Therapists' Lives* (ed: Marcia Hill) Harrington Park Press, an imprint of The Haworth Press, Inc., 1997, pp. 97-100. Single or multiple copies of this article are available for a fee from The Haworth Document Delivery Service [1-800-342-9678, 9:00 a.m. - 5:00 p.m. (EST). E-mail address: getinfo@haworth.com].

imposing my agenda. As much as I knew these issues were important I also adhered to the view that therapy was the context for change, not for instruction. So my conversations with my male clients on these issues were never very satisfactory and I always left feeling I had held back and that we were both missing something. My task became, as Virginia Goldner (1988) states in her article *Generation and Gender: Normative and Covert Hierarchies,* "How can we make the sexual politics of observed and observing systems a subject for therapeutic conversation?" (p. 29).

I believe my desire to improve my therapy with male clients was triggered partly by having my first and only son after raising two girls. I grew up in a family with only sisters as my siblings. It became important for me to see the possibilities of individual change and to develop a more compassionate view towards men's struggles with the social constraints that limit them. During this time I began to be interested in narrative therapy and postmodern theories. The ideas and practices that I began reading about confirmed and validated my current understanding about therapy and shared many concepts with feminist therapy. In particular, they both address power structures and underlying behavior as well as challenge the internalization of dominant norms rather than see problems only in terms of personal pathology. My work with men changed quite naturally as I began to integrate some of the concepts into my current work.

I first began working with my clients to externalize their problems and trace the past, present and future influence of those problems on their lives. By externalizing, the focus of a problem moves from inside the person to outside with a personality all its own. The person begins a process of separation from the dominant stories that have ruled his/her life. The therapist also moves into a relationship with the client to challenge what has been restraining her/him. The client is not fighting against him/herself, as the problem is not inside the client and the therapist is on the same side as the client. There is no convincing and therefore no resistance.

By viewing the problem in this way and maintaining a stance of curiosity about my client's story, that is, coming into sessions to discover stories rather than having stories, I was freed from my old constraints. For example, a concern frequently raised by male clients are the conflicts around being "the provider." By externalizing "the provider" the conversation easily moves into stories about "blueprints" for being a man–their pros and cons and possible alternatives. What I may be curious about as I listen to my client is the history of his relationship with the beliefs and practices of "the provider"; the influence it has had on him; the effects of these beliefs and practices; how they may have interrelated with other beliefs and what may be the tactics or strategies of "the provider." The questions I may ask could include variations on the following:

- How was "the provider" defined in your family?
- What were the advantages and disadvantages to the person occupying this role?
- Would everyone in your family answer in the same way?
- How have these "provider" ideas and practices influenced your life?
  - * How do they direct you?
  - * What may they have stolen from you?
  - * What do they tell you about yourself? Your partner? Your children? Your work?
- Are these ideas working well for you?
- If "the provider" ideas weren't dictating your views, how would things be different?

By asking these types of questions I am able to encourage accountability without blame, and support change rather than imposing it. (These questions are not meant to be prescriptive and would be adapted to individual situations.)

In the process of learning about my clients' beliefs about gender, power, equality, change, love, etc., I also began to question my own stereotypic beliefs and wonder how they might be interfering in my therapy. An important component of the postmodern approach to therapy are the ethical considerations that shape the therapeutic relationship. According to Freedman and Combs in their new book *Narrative Therapy: The Social Construction of Preferred Realities* (1996) these are:

A shift to making room for marginalized voices and marginalized cultures, a shift to people in the client position choosing what fits for them, a shift to therapists being clear where we stand so that people know how to take our ideas, and a shift to considering both the local, interpersonal moment-by-moment effects of our stands and practices and the ripples that those effects send into the world at large. (p. 265)

This, of course, means the therapist must increase her understanding of her own beliefs and be clear about what she expects and how she conceptualizes her therapeutic task. One way that I have attempted to make my ideas about men and therapy more available to my clients is to start by acknowledging that as a woman it is possible that I may not understand some of my male clients' experiences. I want my client to know that I am aware there are things I may not know or "get" and I will check in with him if I notice that happening. I also invite him to point out any time he feels I may be misunderstanding his experience. Frequently this provides opportunities to discuss some of his ideas about having a female therapist, whether this was his preference and why, and what his expectations may be of a female versus a male therapist. Since the gendered beliefs of both the client and therapist are inevitable in the therapy room, approaching our clients in this manner seems to me to be a positive step in overcoming our "hidden" beliefs and behaviors that inhibit clinical progress. I must add that the best parts for me are how much I now enjoy my conversations with my male clients and how much I have learned about them in the process.

REFERENCES

Freedman, J., & Combs, G. (1996). *Narrative therapy: The social construction of preferred realities*. New York, NY: W.W. Norton & Co.

Goldner, V. (1988). Generation and Gender: Normative and Covert Hierarchies. *Family Process, 27*:17-31.

Traumatic Therapy:
How Helping Rape Victims
Affects Me as a Therapist

Millie C. Astin

SUMMARY. The personal experience of treating rape victims is discussed in this paper from the perspective of vicarious traumatization and information processing theory. In particular, symptoms experienced by the rape therapist and challenges to her schemas about the world and others are explored. Suggestions for dealing with vicarious traumatization are included. *[Article copies available for a fee from The Haworth Document Delivery Service: 1-800-342-9678. E-mail address: getinfo@haworth.com]*

As a trauma researcher and therapist, I am regularly faced with hearing graphic details of horrendous experiences. Many in the trauma field have become interested in recent years in the impact this has on therapists. Known as vicarious or secondary traumatization, McCann and Pearlman (1990a) suggest that it is a broader construct than either burnout or coun-

Millie C. Astin, PhD, is Assistant Research Professor at the University of Missouri-St. Louis. She serves as a project director and therapist for a 5-year study funded by NIMH (Principal Investigator: Patricia A. Resick, PhD) to compare cognitive-behavioral treatments for rape victims.

Address correspondence to: Millie Astin, PhD, Department of Psychology, University of Missouri-St. Louis, 8001 Natural Bridge Road, St. Louis, MO 63121-4499.

[Haworth co-indexing entry note]: "Traumatic Therapy: How Helping Rape Victims Affects Me as a Therapist." Astin, Millie C. Co-published simultaneously in *Women & Therapy* (The Haworth Press, Inc.) Vol. 20, No. 1, 1997, pp. 101-109; and: *More than a Mirror: How Clients Influence Therapists' Lives* (ed: Marcia Hill) Harrington Park Press, an imprint of The Haworth Press, Inc., 1997, pp. 101-109. Single or multiple copies of this article are available for a fee from The Haworth Document Delivery Service [1-800-342-9678, 9:00 a.m. - 5:00 p.m. (EST). E-mail address: getinfo@haworth.com].

tertransference. In burnout, the therapist becomes emotionally or psychologically drained due to the toll taken by continuous empathizing and working with difficult clients. In countertransference, unresolved issues of the therapist may be elicited by the client's issues. Of course, vicarious traumatization may include both burnout and countertransference. The latter may be a particular danger when the therapist has his or her own trauma history that has not been dealt with sufficiently (Chrestman, Duncan-Davis, Sullivan, & Kamen, 1994).

While most therapists hear difficult material and occasionally may hear something disgusting or even traumatizing from clients, the trauma therapist, in contrast, gets a steady diet of the traumatic experiences of his or her clients. The therapist's life may not be threatened and no bodily injury occurs. Nevertheless, the trauma therapist may experience symptoms similar to the posttraumatic stress disorder (PTSD) symptoms experienced by trauma survivors. Nightmares, intrusive thoughts, sleep disturbance, irritability, hypervigilance, and emotional numbing are not uncommon among many trauma therapists (Chrestman et al., 1994). Furthermore, the trauma therapist may have to struggle with the challenges to his or her worldview precipitated by the realities of the traumatic experience. Janoff-Bulman (1992) and Epstein (1989) have both argued that when people experience traumatic stressors, their basic assumptions about the world, others, and the self are disrupted. Hearing about traumatic experiences, especially interpersonal traumas in which one person or group of persons inflicts the trauma on another person, defies a view of the world and others as just or good. Thus, depending upon the degree of discrepancy between therapist's schemas and the client's trauma memory, the therapist's schemas may also be disrupted (McCann & Pearlman, 1990a).

Although I have worked with several types of trauma survivors including battered women, childhood sexual and physical abuse survivors, and various other crime victims (e.g., bank robbery victims, etc.), vicarious traumatization never seemed to be an issue for me. Despite hearing the sad and frightening stories of many women who were brutally beaten by their partners, I never took their stories home with me. There were no nightmares about a lover battering my body and breaking my spirit. I never looked over my shoulder to see who might be following me (at least not any more than the average female urbanite). Even though I felt angry about their experiences, I never was tempted to view all men as potential batterers. Similarly with adult survivors of childhood abuse, I felt compassion for them, but there were no moments when I saw a flash of what had happened to them as if it were happening to me. I did not feel detached from others and my sleep was not restless or troubled. However, I didn't think much about the fact that I could leave their stories at the office. Maybe, after all, I was just incredibly well-adjusted.

When the main focus of my work shifted to working with rape victims, that bubble was burst rather quickly. Suddenly, I found myself experiencing nightmares of being raped. Or I would turn a dark corner in my home and imagine a rapist coming toward me just like he had for my client. The more clients I had, the less sleep I got. I found myself becoming tense and irritable. I began to take extra safety precautions and began to view others, especially men, more circumspectly. In short, hearing other women tell me about how they were sexually assaulted was, in small ways, traumatizing and disruptive for me.

As part of a federally-funded treatment outcome study of rape victims, my colleagues and I are comparing two types of treatments for rape victims with posttraumatic stress disorder (PTSD). One is a behavioral treatment called Prolonged Exposure (PE) which was first applied to rape victims by Foa, Rothbaum, Riggs, and Murdock (1991). The other, Cognitive Processing Therapy (CPT), is primarily a cognitive approach, but includes a brief exposure component as well. Based on the strategies of Beckian cognitive therapy (Beck & Emery, 1985; Beck, Rush, Shaw, & Emery, 1979), Resick and Schnicke (1992; 1993) developed and applied this treatment for rape victims.

Both treatments use an information processing model to explain the development and maintenance of PTSD symptoms. Information processing is about how we encode and store information in memory in a format that is useful and easily retrieved. Schemas, for example, are used to facilitate information processing by serving as guides for how to understand a given event or situation (Williams, Watts, MacLeod, & Mathews, 1988). Some have theorized, in this context, that intrusive memories are a normal attempt to process a traumatic event. Traumatic experiences are not easily processed, however, because of the painful and potent emotions (e.g., fear, disgust, humiliation, anger, etc.) associated with the trauma (Foa, Steketee, & Rothbaum, 1989; Resick & Schnicke, 1993). Furthermore, intrusive memories not only elicit overwhelming feelings, but also increase physiological arousal because of the danger associated with the trauma memory. Because the feelings and arousal symptoms are intensely aversive, the individual begins to avoid the memories, feelings, and situations associated with the trauma. Avoidance behaviors temporarily provide relief, but the trauma memory continues to intrude and cause distress because the event has never been processed and incorporated into memory in a meaningful and helpful way. Thus, PTSD symptoms become entrenched. Although this is a cognitive-behavioral explanation of PTSD, it is quite similar to the psychodynamic model proposed by Horowitz (1986) which conceptualizes intrusive memories as a completion tendency to master the trauma and avoidance behaviors as defense mechanisms employed to deal with the painful affect associated with the memories.

Since both Cognitive Processing Therapy and Prolonged Exposure target avoidance as the source of symptom maintenance and interference with processing the trauma, both aim to help the client stop avoiding the trauma memory so that it and the associated emotions can be processed and resolved. Both expect that changes in cognitive schemata will take place. However, PE does not address cognitions directly. Any changes must occur spontaneously as the client adequately processes the trauma and associated affect. CPT, on the other hand, specifically addresses and challenges problematic cognitions that have developed or become entrenched since the rape. Because CPT explicitly outlines these problematic cognitions, I will use a CPT model to delineate my own experience of vicarious traumatization, especially with respect to the cognitive changes I have been confronted with while treating rape survivors.

Just World Theory as developed by Lerner and Miller (1978) states that most people have a belief or schema that the world is just and fair. In other words, good things happen to good people and bad things happen to bad people. A person who experiences a trauma and who endorses this belief will be left without a meaningful way to understand or process the trauma because it does not fit into their schema of the world, others, and herself. Hollon and Garber (1988) have suggested that when an individual is confronted with a schema-discrepant event, the individual can either change or reinterpret the event so that it is congruent with schemas (assimilation) or alter schemata to incorporate the new information provided by the event (accommodation). In most instances, accommodation is the more appropriate response because it takes the new information into account. However, Resick and Schnicke (1992) suggest that rape victims tend to overaccommodate. In other words, they change their beliefs too much.

Thus, when a woman is raped, she is confronted with an event for which she either has no schema or which is inconsistent with preexisting schemas. For example, if she believed on some level that bad things only happen to bad people and she has now been raped, she must either undo the rape or alter her beliefs in some fashion in order to make her experience and schemas congruent. Many women alter the event in some way so that it is no longer interpreted as a rape, and therefore, no longer incongruent with their beliefs. In other words, if something bad did not happen to them, there is no longer a discrepancy to be resolved. Some women minimize the rape ("it wasn't all that bad") or do not label the event as a rape ("he just wanted sex when I didn't–no big deal"). Others blame themselves. Through a series of quasi-logical if-then statements, the rape survivor is able to do away with the rape at her own expense. The reasoning often goes something like the following: (1) "If a particular behavior of mine caused the rape, and (2) if I had not done that, (3) then the rape would not have taken place. (4) Therefore, it was not really a rape because I had control of whether the rape happened or not." Although self-blame is a terrible price to pay, for many rape survivors it is easier than giving up the safety and comfort of their worldview. Of course, if the worldview is acknowledged to be inaccurate, it means that something bad could happen again, which for many is an intolerable thought.

As a rape therapist, my worldview is challenged by the stories of my clients. Intellectually, I know that bad things do happen to good people, yet a part of me clings to a rosy view of the world. Usually, it is abundantly clear that what happened was indeed a rape (nonconsensual sex) even when my client is unsure. Moreover, it is a given that the client did not *cause* the rape whatever her logic might tell her or whatever behaviors she has engaged in which may have made her more vulnerable to being raped. A rape occurs when the rapist chooses a victim, not when the victim does something that precipitates the rape. Despite my desire to hang on to a safe world, I never struggle with the victim's story here. Instead, it is at another point that many of my clients get stuck, and that I also get stuck. Not only do clients blame themselves for causing the rape, but also for behaviors during the rape that conceivably might have altered the course of events. "If only I had fought back. If only I had screamed so that others nearby would have come to my rescue. If only I had not lay there frozen, doing nothing."

Sometimes, it is obvious that their expectations are unrealistic. Most women cannot overpower or outrun a male assailant. It is just as likely that fighting back could have resulted in greater violence or death and a passive stance may be the one that allowed the victim to survive. Other expectations may be more realistic. I find myself thinking, "Why didn't you scream when you knew people were nearby?" or "How could you have chosen not to even tell him to stop?" I know the answers, but always have to go over them in my head to convince myself. The truth is people in danger sometimes freeze just like the rabbit in the car headlights. If she ran, she *might* survive, but fear has frozen her in place. And even if she had not been frozen, no one knows if it would have helped or made the situation worse. Intellectually, the answer is satisfying to me, but on a more visceral level, I find it unacceptable. If I accept this reality, I have to give up my notion of my own invulnerability and my competence to take care of myself. My schemas are challenged. I don't want to contemplate the possibility that I, too, might freeze or be unable to do anything to rectify the situation. It goes against my cherished notion that whatever bad comes my way, I will be able to handle it and overcome it. Each time I help a client accept her vulnerability and the fact that she "just froze," I have to accept that possibility for myself. I don't like it and resist it every time.

The other thing that people do when an event is incongruent with their beliefs is to change their beliefs. In fact, CPT aims to help clients accommodate or change their belief systems. Instead of "bad things happen only to bad people," we hope to see them incorporate their experience and conclude that "bad things can happen to anyone." Instead of "everyone can be trusted," we look for "some people can be trusted and others cannot be trusted." Unfortunately, rape victims tend to overaccommodate. "Bad things *always* happen to good people." "No one can be trusted." "I cannot be hurt" becomes "I will be hurt again and again."

In CPT, we focus on five areas in which overaccommodation of cognitive schemata are likely to occur. First suggested by McCann and Pearlman (1990b), these include safety, trust, control, esteem, and intimacy. Each can be considered in terms of the self or others. For example, a rape victim might have difficulty trusting others, especially men. On the other hand, she might have trouble trusting herself or her own judgement if she thought the person was trustworthy or that her situation was safe. As I work with rape survivors, I have found the cognitive changes associated with overaccommodation to be slow and insidious. I *know* when I am struggling with an assimilation issue. Overaccommodation issues, on the other hand, seem to grow quietly in my psyche until one day I notice that my behaviors and thoughts have changed. Changes in cognitions about others, especially regarding safety, trust, and esteem seem more problematic. Without noting when these changes began to take place, I suddenly find myself more critical of the quality of the locks in my home and replace them with better ones. The car door is always locked when I'm driving. I am more careful with whom I speak in public. I find myself wondering why that guy is walking toward me and clutch my keys ready to strike out if I have to. I question the motives of others much more readily and never assume they mean me no harm.

One day I was at home ill and because I had not gone out, I had left the screen door as well as the front door locked. This prevented the postal carrier from slipping my mail through my door slot and he left a note to that effect. Later on, a neighbor came by to visit me and read the note and when he saw me, laughingly asked what kind of [crazy] person would lock their screen door. I felt a flush of anger and thought to myself, "someone who knows bad things can happen to her, that the world is not safe, and that not everyone can be trusted."

Of course, there is a positive side. My rape clients have given me a great gift without knowing it. Without ever having to be traumatized myself, I have learned precisely those things. Bad things *can* happen to me, there *is* danger out there, not everyone *can* be trusted. That is accommodation. As a result, I don't live in a fantasy world and I take active steps to reduce risk and vulnerability. The danger, the one that I have to fight all the time, is that insidious slide into overaccommodation in which there is *no* goodness in the world or others. When you hear about being raped on a regular basis, it's a very easy shift from knowing that you should not be overly trusting to believing that no one merits trust.

The danger with vicarious traumatization is twofold. Naturally, no one wants to be traumatized, not even someone in a helping profession who cares about victims. I don't want to live with symptoms that disrupt my life. I also don't care for that subtle, almost imperceptible shift into a more cynical, jaded worldview that has the potential to isolate me from others. The other great danger, of course, is that the therapist will become ineffective, or even worse, harmful to the client. If you don't want to give up your worldview, it may be easier to blame the victim or collude with the client in avoiding confrontation of the trauma memory. If you have adopted the client's overaccommodated worldview, it will be next to impossible to help her find the healthier middle ground. Thus, for both professional and personal reasons, vicarious traumatization needs to be recognized and dealt with.

Not every client affects me this way. Some traumas are more difficult to deal with than others. Some clients are more difficult to deal with than others. I feel the strain more during periods when my caseload of rape clients is higher. Fortunately, I have found that a number of things help reduce the effects of vicarious traumatization. Various suggestions have been made about ways to deal with vicarious traumatization. These include balancing trauma and non-trauma clients in your caseload, engaging in a variety of professional tasks other than clinical duties, establishing boundaries between professional and personal activities, and maintaining health through adequate nutrition, rest, and exercise (McCann & Pearlman, 1990a). Most who have written about vicarious traumatization have stressed the importance of practicing what we preach to clients (Figley, 1995; McCann & Pearlman, 1990a). With that in mind, I don't allow myself to avoid the issue or deny its existence. Nor do I allow myself to keep it to myself. Thankfully, I work with other trauma therapists and have colleagues with whom I can process what I have heard, talk about how it has made me feel, and who will remind me of steps that I can take to deal with the trauma. This is probably the most crucial step and is amazingly powerful in its ability to put the trauma into perspective. Unfortunately, in some settings there is an assumption that a therapist who has trouble with hearing traumas is somehow weak or inadequate or has unresolved issues. As stated earlier, unresolved issues may complicate trauma therapy. Nevertheless, the parallel of vicarious traumatization with client victimization should suggest that the primary factor is not the individual, but the trauma itself. To be troubled by hearing the terrible things that one person can do to another is a normal response, but like the client's symptoms, reflect a reaction to a trauma experience.

The second thing that I find helpful is working through my own assumptions and how they have been challenged or altered by listening to traumas. I try to review my assumptions regularly, especially when I observe a new behavior or attitude in myself. If necessary, I will challenge my assumptions if they appear unrealistic. McCann and Pearlman (1990a) state that alterations in the trauma therapist's cognitions are probably inevitable. You cannot listen to trauma stories and maintain a naively positive worldview unless you choose to blame the victims. As I have indicated, though such changes can be painful because they elucidate your own vulnerability, they can be positive in that you have the opportunity to live more realistically. The more difficult challenge is to maintain a stance that allows you to incorporate realistically positive and negative views of the world and others without sliding into an overaccommodated perspective.

When I first began working with rape victims, I found it puzzling that I experienced some symptoms of vicarious traumatization, but had never experienced this while working with other victims. As I thought about it, I came to realize that with other victims I had been able to set myself apart from them and maintain my sense of invulnerability. "Perhaps that client was abused as a child, but I am an adult and it can't happen to me." "Maybe she got caught up in an abusive relationship, but I never have, so it is unlikely that I ever will." (One might debate the latter as an illusion, but on some level, whether accurate or not, it allowed me to maintain a sense of invulnerability.) With rape, I could not maintain my distance. As I helped my clients to see that bad things happen to people randomly, I could no longer keep my invulnerability intact. I was just as vulnerable as anyone else. That realization made me more susceptible to symptoms of vicarious traumatization. It also has brought me closer to the struggles of my clients. For that I am grateful.

REFERENCES

Beck, A.T., & Emery, G. (1985). *Anxiety disorders and phobias.* New York: Basic Books.

Beck, A.T., Rush, A.J., Shaw, B.F., & Emery, G. (1979). *Cognitive therapy of depression.* New York: Guilford Press.

Chrestman, K.R., Duncan-Davis, J., Sullivan, M., & Kamen, D. (1994, November). *Risky business: Primary and secondary traumatization among therapists who work with trauma survivors.* Poster presented at the annual meeting of the International Society for Traumatic Stress Studies, Chicago, IL.

Epstein, S. (1989). The self-concept, the traumatic neurosis, and the structure of personality. In D. Ozer, J.M. Healy, Jr., & A.J. Stewart (Eds.), *Perspectives on personality,* Vol. 3. Greenwich, CT: JAI Press.

Figley, C.R. (Ed.). (1995). *Compassion fatigue: Coping with secondary traumatic stress disorder in those who treat the traumatized.* New York: Brunner/Mazel.

Foa, E.B., Rothbaum, B.O., Riggs, D.S., & Murdock, T.B. (1991). Treatment of posttraumatic stress disorder in rape victims: A comparison between cognitive-behavioral procedures and counseling. *Journal of Consulting and Clinical Psychology, 59,* 715-723.

Foa, E.B., Steketee, G.S., & Rothbaum, B.O. (1989). Behavioral/cognitive conceptualizations of post-traumatic stress disorder. *Behavior Therapy, 20,* 155-176,

Hollon, S.D., & Garber, J. (1988). Cognitive therapy. In L.Y. Abramson (Ed.), *Social cognition and clinical psychology: A synthesis* (pp. 204-253). New York: Guilford.

Horowitz, M.J. (1986). *Stress response syndromes.* North Vale, NJ: Jason Aronson.

Janoff-Bulman, R. (1992). *Shattered assumptions: Toward a new psychology of trauma.* New York: Free Press.

Lerner, M.J., & Miller, D.T. (1978). Just world research and the attribution process: Looking back and ahead. *Psychological Bulletin, 85,* 1030-1051.

McCann, I.L., & Pearlman, L.A. (1990a). Vicarious traumatization: A framework for understanding the psychological effects of working with victims. *Journal of Traumatic Stress, 3,* 131-149.

McCann, I.L., & Pearlman, L.A. (1990b). *Psychological trauma and the adult survivor: Theory, therapy, and transformation.* New York: Brunner/Mazel.

Resick, P.A., & Schnicke, M.K. (1992). Cognitive processing therapy for sexual assault victims. *Journal of Consulting and Clinical Psychology, 60,* 748-756.

Resick, P.A., & Schnicke, M.K. (1993). *Cognitive processing therapy for rape victims: A treatment manual.* Newbury Park, CA: Sage Publications.

Williams, J.M.G., Watts, F.N., MacLeod, C., & Mathews, A. (1988). *Cognitive psychology and emotional disorders.* New York: John Wiley.

Frank Revelations
of a Difficult Therapy Experience:
Countertransference Observations

Melinda Ginne

SUMMARY. A single case history illustrates the dilemma a psychotherapist faces when her social values obstruct the therapeutic alliance. In this case a feminist therapist depicts the countertransference complexities involved in treating a man who appears to be psychologically tormenting his wife. *[Article copies available for a fee from The Haworth Document Delivery Service: 1-800-342-9678. E-mail address: getinfo@haworth.com]*

I recall feeling my way through this case, step by step. At times I would think that I had a grasp on it and at other times I would consider myself hopelessly ensconced in doubts and concerns, unable to see the big picture. I am still not sure if I can identify what I learned from this experience. As I look back on it what looms largest for me is that I survived it. I walked into a psychic minefield with this client, and continue to put the pieces together.

A good friend and colleague called me to request that I see a mid-life man with a drinking problem. My friend was seeing this man and his wife

---

Melinda Ginne holds a doctorate in clinical psychology. She has been a psychotherapist and member of the Feminist Therapist Institute since 1982.

Address correspondence to: Melinda Ginne, PhD, P.O. Box 13061, Oakland, CA 94661.

[Haworth co-indexing entry note]: "Frank Revelations of a Difficult Therapy Experience: Countertransference Observations." Ginne, Melinda. Co-published simultaneously in *Women & Therapy* (The Haworth Press, Inc.) Vol. 20, No. 1, 1997, pp. 111-117; and: *More than a Mirror: How Clients Influence Therapists' Lives* (ed: Marcia Hill) Harrington Park Press, an imprint of The Haworth Press, Inc., 1997, pp. 111-117. Single or multiple copies of this article are available for a fee from The Haworth Document Delivery Service [1-800-342-9678, 9:00 a.m. - 5:00 p.m. (EST). E-mail address: getinfo@haworth.com].

111

in marital therapy. Their marriage was in trouble for reasons beyond the alcohol problem. My colleague did not give many details, but wanted to refer him to me for evaluation and treatment of the substance abuse problem.

When I first saw Bob he was casually but neatly dressed. At about 6'2", he was slender but muscular, with deep olive colored skin, brown penetrating eyes, and salt and pepper gray hair. His appearance seemed studied and premeditated. I remember thinking that he was probably what many people deemed classically handsome, but that there was something cold and distant about him. I felt cautious rather than drawn to him. I was intrigued by a man who intentionally concerned himself with his appearance, had the right natural resources, but somehow lacked appeal. I found myself wondering what he thought about me. I assumed that a man who involved himself with his image would also be alert to the images of others. Although I had a well-designed office in a good part of town, I was certainly less attentive to appearances than Bob might like. I remember noticing his reactions to me and wondering how I would establish rapport.

He told me he was 54 years of age and managed his own business that was doing quite well. He had been a long time Bay Area resident and his business was straight out of the Haight Ashbury tradition. Similarly, like some of his Bay Area baby boomer peers, Bob's early counter-culture endeavors now allowed him dinners at four-star restaurants and box seats at the opera.

In gathering background information I assessed Bob's use of alcohol and other drugs. He described daily marijuana use and wine with dinner three to four times per week. He did not think he used either substance to excess. He did realize that his wife was concerned about his use, and since he wanted to maintain his marriage, he was willing to eliminate all substances and go to Alcoholics Anonymous meetings. Although we spent time in the therapy sessions discussing recovery issues, Bob really wanted to talk about his wife. He felt that she was slipping away from him and he was desperate to keep her. She was 31 years of age and an aspiring actor. They had been married for three years. In the past six months she had been in and out of their home, staying with friends when she and Bob argued.

Early in his treatment Bob had given me permission to consult with the therapist who had originally referred him to me. He reiterated this consent periodically, even after he had stopped attending therapy sessions with his wife. I think he might have believed that he stood a chance of winning his wife back as long as he stayed in therapy and let his wife indirectly hear about it through my consultation with the marital therapist. When I reflect on why Bob came to therapy, I think that one of his primary motives might have been to rekindle his wife's affections by appearing to be exploring his personal problems. When I depict Bob in this way, I infer that I was manipulated by him. I suspect that this was entirely possible. In attending to the overtly dysfunctional aspects of his concerns I probably overlooked some of the underlying dynamics.

Through conversations with the marital therapist I learned about Bob's wife's worries. He had not beaten her or tried to intimidate her but he had been lewd and invasive on several occasions, causing her to be afraid of him. After the second year of marriage, his wife had asked to be able to move some things into a spare bedroom and occasionally sleep there. Although he tried to dissuade her she had prevailed. However, a few days later, while she was at a class, he systematically went through the house removing and destroying all of the doors. He removed the doors to the bedrooms and the bathrooms. His invasion of her privacy prompted her to move out permanently.

As I learned about Bob's brazen behaviors, I felt put off. I wanted him to change. At times I would address this directly. I would tell Bob that his behavior was causing a problem in his marriage and in his ability to relate to women. There were times when he seemed receptive to this advice, but more often he argued his perspective. He construed our discourse as a battle of the sexes, and I often wondered if that was true. I scrutinized my intentions toward Bob and found grounds to doubt my motivations. Was I trying to work through an ambivalence toward men in this treatment? As I looked inside for answers, it was difficult to be conclusive. I did not feel antipathy toward men as a class, and I did not have a need to exercise combative feelings toward men. I do, however, often feel critical of the ways that many men choose to interact with women, and Bob was highly illustrative of the type of man who brings out my sharpest critic. I could not wholeheartedly absolve myself of countertransference motives.

At some point soon thereafter, I asked Bob about the incident with the doors. He admitted that this had occurred, but he did not think that it had much relevance to his marital problems. I thought that his actions were painfully relevant to the negative outcomes in his marriage. I was beginning to realize the extent to which I perceived him to be tormenting his wife with his intrusive behaviors. These were some of the moments in the treatment when I felt the least adequate. I was struggling to offset my disapproving opinions of his behaviors in order to foster a therapeutic alliance. I did not think it would have been helpful to confront his denial directly because our alliance was so fragile. Yet these issues seemed so intense and provocative, I experienced myself as barely hanging on to the reins while Bob drove the horses faster and faster.

I have often wondered about my role in this case. I questioned whether or not it was appropriate for me to want to change him. In my fantasies misogynistic men find feminist therapists who can vitalize their super-egos. On one hand I wanted to overtly direct him, to guide him into change. On the other hand most of my clinical training has cautioned me to follow the client's process, to observe intra-psychic and interpersonal phenomena. Comments upon these perceptions can set the stage for change, but whether or not to work on personal transformation remains the prerogative of the client. I have been trained to set aside my reactions in order to align with diverse clients, and that change occurs within the context of this alignment. Because I could not readily resolve my cognitive dissonance, I found myself vacillating between a genuine desire to be helpful to Bob and an ambivalence toward him. Since I did not know how to use my reactions constructively, I filed them in my mind. I believed that there would be an opening at some point in the therapy when I would be able to insert prescriptions for more appropriate thoughts and behaviors.

One day Bob brought in a set of photos that a professional photographer had taken of his wife. The photos were rather suggestive pictures of his wife wearing low-cut blouses, short skirts and spiked heels. She was bending over so you could see her bosom, or turned in a three-quarters pose to reveal her derriere. I began to think of Bob's marriage differently. I had not realized that my mind had created an engram of a sweeter, more wholesome wife. When he had said she was an actor, I had conjured up Helen Hunt. After seeing her photos, she reminded me more of Jayne Mansfield. I felt chagrined to realize how Pollyanna-ish my images had been, and how on some level I had been ascribing the marital corruption solely to Bob.

In my original conceptualization the marital problems were derivative of developmental and age differences. This paradigm felt familiar to me and allowed me to construct a case formulation that had integrity and created potential for change or growth. I had not been aware of this mechanism until I began to think of it in contrast to my newer, more unsettling thoughts: that there was a sadistic and voyeuristic aspect to this marriage, and that this, in fact, was the focus of treatment.

I am not so prim and proper that I am unable to entertain paraphilic thoughts, tendencies, or behaviors, in myself or in my clients. However, I had not taken this case with that understanding. I think there was something about the way the case unfolded that kept me feeling as if I was walking down a dark street without a road map. There were surprises at every turn, and I was not so sure that I trusted Bob enough to let him be the tour guide, or that I liked him enough to want to go where he was going. I continued to take the position that he was supposed to lead the therapy.

Bob wanted to possess his wife and because he could not, he devised an opportunity to steer her away from her acting career, which he found threatening. She had not been able to make a living at her career so he supported her. He now proposed to establish her in a business, an offer she could not refuse. They agreed to open a small boutique near their home. Over time I came to understand that he had strategically tied up all of their assets so that if she were to proceed with a divorce she would not benefit financially. He had arranged their finances in such a way that she was bound to the small boutique for all of her liquid resources. If she were to divorce him he would retain the business and she would be destitute.

Bob was more methodical than I had perceived. As I saw more of how his mind worked I grew increasingly doubtful about my ability to remain impartial or fair-minded. I suppose I thought I could inculcate him with what I considered to be principles of decency. My maneuvering did not evade him. He responded by playing cat and mouse with me, laying out provocative (read: anti-feminist) situations in his life and scrutinizing my reactions. Theoretically, this could be considered ideal transference mate-rial, but I could not forestall my own discomfort sufficiently to utilize the transference effectively in the sessions.

Bob's compulsive behaviors continued to reveal themselves. He was going by his wife's shop and walking into the store while customers were there. He would stand there watching her intently, causing her customers to feel distressed. Eventually she called him and asked him to stop coming to the shop, but as she had no leverage, he continued to do as he pleased.

He would detail these occurrences during the therapy hour and I would try to redirect him to a more socially appropriate solution. He grew to openly dispute my advice. I examined the parallels between his wife and myself. He was also coming into my "shop" and I felt uneasy, and I thought I had no leverage to get him to leave my shop. As a fee-for-service client, I was, to some extent, dependent on him. I think that like his wife, I felt trapped and dependent.

I tried to understand why I felt stymied. My thoughts led to three primary conclusions. First, I had more than fifteen years of professional experience and I liked to think of myself as an effective therapist. Since I was not feeling competent at this stage of the therapy, I was unwilling to let go. I did not want to walk away from this therapy presuming that I did not know what direction to take and that I had lost my confidence. Second-ly, I wanted the friend and colleague who had referred Bob to me to think of me as a skilled therapist. She was someone I greatly admired, especially for her ability to work effectively with all types of clients and to maintain her goodwill consistently toward them. I felt ashamed to admit that there were times when I felt mired in negative thoughts about Bob. Lastly, I wanted Bob to change. I wanted him to be less lecherous, more trustworthy, and more insightful. I wanted him to become a man a person could rely upon.

Although I had relatively little contact with the therapist who had referred Bob to me, I did get another call from her when Bob's wife was going to divorce him. Her car had been broken into, she was frightened, and she was convinced that Bob had done it. She felt she had to sever all ties with him. Once his wife filed for divorce she moved out of the state. The therapy continued for two to three more months; however, it was essentially null and void. It consisted of a few half-hearted attempts on his part to engage me by reporting provocative material, and my attempts to provide education and socialization, which he resisted.

I sought out several consultations from colleagues and thoroughly explored my legal obligations in this case. Although Bob's behavior leaned toward the illegal, he was well within legal bounds as far as my reporting responsibilities were concerned. His wife could have pursued burglary charges for the car theft and requested a restraining order. I believe that ultimately, considering the constraints of the legal and therapeutic systems, she did the best she could, by cutting her losses and moving on with her life.

I really did not figure my way out of the therapy. In the end it was Bob who found a way out of the treatment. One day he came to therapy and announced that he had found a Jungian therapist he liked and he was going to start seeing her. In most other cases I do not accept a transition like this very readily. I often want to explore termination in therapy and complete any unfinished business. However, I only felt great relief. I considered getting his permission to contact his new therapist to help him segue from one therapy to another, but he refused permission.

When I look back on this case, I think that there are times in treatment when we do our best to gauge the rapport in order to know if we can present thoughts and reflections that our clients might find anxiety provoking. There are times when we do not know if the motivation for our interventions arises from our genuine goodwill for our client or from a desire to allay our discomfort with their behaviors. Did I want Bob to prosper in the way that he was perceiving life and conducting his interpersonal relations? No. Was I clear enough in pointing out drawbacks to his behavior and showing him more appropriate examples? I believe that I was. Was it countertransference that resulted in a desire to change him in ways that he did not ask for or want? I am still not sure. I do think that the crux of the countertransference is found in the tension between my feminist ideology and my obligation as a clinician to suspend my beliefs in order to align with the client. Having a limited capacity to enter into a genuine alliance with this client restrained the range and effectiveness of my interactions with him and ultimately diluted the interventions I presented to him.

Parallel Process:
Client and Therapist Explore Motherloss

Cathy R. Hauer

SUMMARY. This article addresses parallel processes between the author (a therapist) and client when each are mourning the death of their mother. Similarities and differences in their experience and reaction are discussed. The effect of the client's unexpressed grief from her early childhood loss is explored. The author also examines her own, more recent loss and develops a new perspective on its consequences. Tools are presented to help the client work on her grief, especially when the issue is "motherloss." The impact of the therapeutic process on the client and author is delineated, and the client's reactions to ending her therapy are analyzed. *[Article copies available for a fee from The Haworth Document Delivery Service: 1-800-342-9678. E-mail address: getinfo@haworth.com]*

When I got the call from a former client I had seen briefly in lesbian couples therapy (she and her partner were separating), I never imagined

Cathy R. Hauer, MS, is a licensed psychotherapist in private practice in Northern California. As an educator and trainer, she has spoken on women's issues, diversity, disability awareness and HIV/AIDS. As a clinician, she sees clients with a variety of issues including coming out, chronic illness and grief/loss. She is especially interested in exploring "motherloss" issues with colleagues and welcomes comments. Additionally, she is on the Board of Directors of the Santa Clara Valley Chapter of the California Association of Marriage & Family Therapists.

Address correspondence to: Cathy Hauer, MS, MFCC, P.O. Box 2426, El Granada, CA 94018.

[Haworth co-indexing entry note]: "Parallel Process: Client and Therapist Explore Motherloss." Hauer, Cathy R.. Co-published simultaneously in *Women & Therapy* (The Haworth Press, Inc.) Vol. 20, No. 1, 1997, pp. 119-126; and: *More than a Mirror: How Clients Influence Therapists' Lives* (ed: Marcia Hill) Harrington Park Press, an imprint of The Haworth Press, Inc., 1997, pp. 119-126. Single or multiple copies of this article are available for a fee from The Haworth Document Delivery Service [1-800-342-9678, 9:00 a.m. - 5:00 p.m. (EST). E-mail address: getinfo@haworth.com].

119

the intense internal process of my own which would unfold as we worked together. "Laura" was now wanting to start individual work with me, more than a year later, to explore her issues around the new relationship, and especially to look at her fears about intimacy that were surfacing.

The transference potential was there from the start, and I was soon to see that the countertransference road was also laid out well. Laura had originally sought me out because I had advertised as a lesbian feminist therapist. She had obviously felt some connection with me from our brief previous work, and so was reaching out again for help. We were both in our mid-30s (although she may not have been aware of how close in age we were), worked in similar professions and were both in relationships. She was just finishing up her last year of social work graduate school and was in a new and for her very different relationship with "Deanna," yet felt the potential to pull back from this good relationship if she didn't confront what was going on for her.

Laura was not at first able to articulate exactly what was happening, only that she was reacting to Deanna's expressions of closeness by wanting to push her away. The fact of her mother's death when Laura was ten had not been discussed during our previous couples work. However, it came up early on in our individual work, and I quickly sensed that I was in for a challenge, as my mother had died several years before and I was still very much in a grieving process, exploring this sense of what I called "motherloss." This was just a year or two before several good books on the topic were published (Edelman, 1994; Vozenilek, Ed., 1992).

Although Laura had not initially sought therapy to talk about her motherloss issues, we soon agreed that much of what she was dealing with did indeed relate to that early experience. She presented in therapy wanting to explore issues of dependence, neediness and abandonment. As she shared her memories of how her mother's death was handled, she also talked about all the truly positive and enriching aspects of her current situation. Interestingly, her manner of presentation did not seem to indicate regard for these parts of her life as fulfilling. I was aware that Laura seemed unable to internalize anything positive about her life in the present tense. Laura's affect from the beginning of our work together was blunted and she always slouched down on the couch. I had to stop myself from pursuing the goal of getting her to sit up straight, as desirable as that might have been. What was interesting to me was that, regardless of her successes in school, at her internship, in a community volunteer position, and in a good relationship, Laura was unable to hold internally a consistently positive image of herself. She described that on the job she was unable to "pump up her ego herself."

Laura came to realize that, in her approach to life and relationships, the internal monologue was, "If a person really loves me, they'll die; if things go well, tragedy will strike." She even found it hard to believe someone would love her at all. Additionally, she carried a sense of shame; "I must have done something wrong and then my mother died." This translated into a generalized and vague feeling that she had made a big mistake and would get caught. Predictably, she self-described as a perfectionist, and always felt like she was faking it. Laura also detested being complimented and cringed whenever someone was sympathetic toward her. I came to feel that what Laura was missing was an inner sense of "mother support." The discrepancy between objectively positive experiences in real life and her subjective interpretations of same, led me to focus on her very early and painful loss and especially on how she had been unable then (and was still unable) to make any sense of the loss. Hers was a particularly painful one and was mishandled by her family.

Laura was never given an opportunity to mourn her mother's death, nor understand it, as a child or as an adult. Her mother had been sick for some time with breast cancer (at a time when cancer was spoken of in hushed tones and never to children), had been in and out of the hospital and was in the hospital around the time of Laura's tenth birthday and her trip to sleep-away summer camp. Before her birthday party and departure, her mother died but her family decided not to tell her anything. She left and returned after two weeks to find her bedroom redecorated and her mother gone. The funeral took place without her, and her family (father, aunt, much older sister) was basically unable to discuss anything with Laura. Much of the work we did together revolved around the important processes of grieving and mourning. Because this had not been done at the time with her family, she felt she had neither the understanding of nor the tools with which to approach the task.

When I first realized that Laura and I had experienced and were both still experiencing a similarly profound sense of loss, anguish, deep sadness and feelings of being bereft and abandoned, I began thinking about the nature of motherloss from a new perspective. How could my reactions so closely resemble hers when the circumstances, not to mention our ages at our mothers' deaths, were so different? I began to see that losing a parent, particularly one's mother, especially perhaps a female losing her mother, can evoke a wrenching disconnection which permeates all aspects of our lives and stays with us, in spite of the message to get on with it. I also saw that, in addition to a mutually loving and caring relationship with my mother, one unfinished aspect for us had elements of childhood dependence and unresolved needs (which I was literally about to confront her with when she was diagnosed with cancer). This led me to seek some very specific ways to address this internal conflict for myself.

In my own therapy I explored the depth of my feelings of loss, struggling, at times, to remember the crucial differences between my issues and those of my client. I *did* have an internalized mother support system and I had *not* been ten when she died. Unlike my client, my childhood had not been disrupted by watching a mother becoming increasingly ill with cancer at a time when her attention, care and love were especially needed and she was unable to give it. The fact that my subjective experience of this loss sometimes felt that way gave me a lot to think about; ultimately these juxtaposed situations helped me to put mine in a more realistic perspective. Around that time I attended an ongoing workshop for women called "Mourning and Mitzvah" which helped me immensely through writing projects and group discussions. The leader later published her materials as a workbook (Brener, 1993).

As I heard Laura talk about her feelings around her mother's death, and as they closely mirrored my own, naturally my empathy rose strongly in my heart and I worked hard to keep her experience separate from mine. Being someone whose eyes tear up easily when touched by expressions of pain, I really had to watch my reactions so as not to distract her from her process. I also decided early on that I needed to refrain from self-disclosing about my own experience around parent loss. I chose not to disclose because I was absolutely sure that I would cry while talking about my own loss, and felt that the following scenario would probably ensue: Laura, comfortable showing empathy toward others but not toward herself, would then outwardly show concern for me, thereby cutting off her own feelings of grief and despair. Resentment for the distraction would probably follow, and our process would be interrupted, even derailed.

The other area where my client and I had somewhat similar issues was about commitment. Laura's loving feelings in her current relationship with Deanna were constantly being countered by a sense of wanting to flee when Deanna got close (physically and emotionally), which Laura perceived as Deanna being "needy." Laura also had very rigid ways of seeing things at work and needed to control many situations. As she began to talk about this, we started what I called "heavy digging." I soon realized we were each doing digging of our own! Of course, this brought up some anxiety for me. Throughout my years in private practice, I have certainly been touched by my clients' stories, and challenged by both similarities to and differences from my own experiences. This time, though, I was affected on a deeply personal level. At first I thought the only connection would be the issue of motherloss, which was painful enough. Soon, however, I was to see that my issues about relationships were being triggered as well. Since in my training and experience I hadn't heard many therapists talk about this, I felt somewhat out of my element. Even writing about it now is a wonderful yet risky antidote to the typical silence in our profession about these very real aspects of the therapeutic process. This article, being a synthesis of our actual two years together and the ways in which our processes ran parallel, can only present one or two dimensions of what was definitely a three-dimensional experience.

As Laura told me more about her ambivalent feelings in what sounded like a healthy relationship, I reflected on my own situation, and the progression I experienced moving into a deeper commitment. I was six years into a solid relationship (my first long-term, committed one) and some demons of my own occasionally surfaced around intimacy and ambivalence which I was confronting in my own therapy. My partner/spouse (we're all looking for better words for this, I know) astutely suggested that this demon was related to my mother's untimely death, which had occurred just eighteen months into our own relationship. I do sometimes characterize our first year before my mother's cancer diagnosis as different. That difference was not simply a matter of having been in the early amorous stage of the relationship.

Prior to my mom's death, I had an overall feeling of safety in the world. This was in spite of my parents divorcing when I was eleven, or having been on the receiving end of various crimes (bicycles and a car stolen, and apartment break-in). I felt secure, and had not yet dealt directly with the death of someone close to me, although people I knew had died throughout my life, even a close family friend. I would say that I had not truly experienced death, and certainly not grieving. My entire essence shifted after her death, my stance in the world changed and my feelings of safety and security were, if not permanently shattered, then significantly altered for good. Things that wouldn't have previously devastated me, now did. I found myself sobbing after a "scary" amusement park ride, and crying as if my heart would break when I found a dead baby bird outside my house. Trusting in this good, solid relationship was a challenge and I heard my own internal monologue of "If I love you, you'll die." This surprised me, as I hadn't thought of myself as having so-called intimacy issues. However, clearly there was fear and anxiety on my part to be fully present in this relationship. In my work with this client, I wanted to help her develop a context for her similar feelings and to make some sense of them, even as I was doing so for myself.

We looked at Laura's rigidity, fear and discomfort around connecting with loved ones and really being seen as a worthy individual, and how all of that affected her daily life, decisions and reactions. She never wanted to "be the fool" and didn't want to get excited about anything lest it be taken away or lost. She didn't want to tell Deanna that she missed her (when they were apart on business trips) because then she was sure Deanna would "latch on to" her. Further digging revealed that feeling vulnerable brought such anxiety that it was to be avoided at all costs. A poignant memory was of climbing into her mother's lap, only to be taken off, because it hurt her mother too much. Laura also interpreted much of Deanna's intimacy with her as "taking something from" Laura, which is a rich image, especially if you think about where Laura's mother is in that picture. Laura realized that she often reacted to Deanna in ways like the hurt, betrayed ten-year-old, with fear, and wanting desperately to withdraw and cling at the same time. She was also uncomfortable telling Deanna that she loved her.

Fortunately, because Laura was earnest in confronting these issues, and consistent in her sessions, insights came pouring forth from her, and she seriously mulled over suggestions and interpretations from me. At the same time, watching her put together this puzzle from pieces which she had not previously named or described allowed me an unexpected bonus. I began to step away from my own grieving process enough to believe the notion that I had been telling her: healing is possible. It was as if by watching her take a new perspective on her life through understanding the effect of not just her mother's death but the way it was handled, I was able to do the same for myself in spite of the very different circumstances. My sense of having been devastated by my loss changed as I heard more about her loss, and in a sense, my strength grew as I saw hers grow.

During the time we worked together, Laura started a good post-graduate job at a social service agency, moved in with Deanna, and had a lovely commitment ceremony. She started opening up more with Deanna and was better able to communicate her deepest feelings. Slouching low on the couch, though, seemed to be her natural position, as that had not changed over time, even when she did begin to show a wider range of emotions in therapy and at home with Deanna. To help her focus on issues of loss, I suggested that Laura look at some books about death and grieving, including children's books. I brought in *Talking about Death* (Grollman, 1990) and read the children's story from it, and she cried. We talked about the possibility of Deanna reading her a story and comforting her. At first Laura balked at this idea, but stayed true to her commitment to this process. When they read the story together, they both cried. Laura got through the unbearable feelings that came up anytime Deanna comforted her, feelings which were so caught up in a paradoxical loop: she's terribly uncomfortable being comforted because she never got the comforting she needed because her mother was gone when she needed her most. This rang true for me, too, as I later wrote in a poem, "Who would teach her how to be with the dying/the one who was dying?"

About a year and a half into our work together, the question arose: "So, is this grief stuff always going to be here?" Laura had thought, of course, that we'd get *done* with it and that would be that. And so we moved into the last phase of therapy for her, helping develop a literal and figurative way to put this to rest, but also to acknowledge that yes, it will always be here but not in the heavy, burdensome ways that it had been. We talked about the image of a room (a mother-room) from which she can exit and then return to, having filled it with memories (some of which she had only voiced for the first time in therapy) and both happy and sad feelings. Until then, she had been stuck in the dark with no memories, no pictures, nothing to hold onto. Laura came up with the idea of making a picture collage, and set about contacting her sister and aunt for contributions. This project was very comforting (her word!) to her.

I was aware at this point of how having been through my own similar process gave me many useful ideas to share with her, and an understanding of the need to do quantifiable grief work. In general, this can be anything with a goal of really experiencing the pain of mourning (which works well in conjunction with support groups and individual therapy): a picture project like Laura chose, reading books on the subject (especially ones written for children), guided imagery, workshops, connecting with family members and good friends of the person who died, writing "to" them, creating a "memorial" or altar of pictures and memorabilia of the person, lighting a candle in their honor on the anniversary of their death, learning different spiritual mourning practices. Doing some of these myself (plus therapy and reflecting on my work with this particular client) allowed me to move from an overwhelming sense of "How could this happen to me" to "What can I learn from this; how can I grow through this?" Instead of seeing my loss as a terrible burden of pain, I found ways to see it as a gift, and felt more able to survive anything and live through it. Time is, of course, a great healer. As year after passing year is marked with the lighting of a *Yarzheit* candle for my mother, I know that I am another year stronger.

Soon afterward, Laura talked about feeling ready to set a date for ending therapy. Seeing a possibility for a negative transference experience, I reinforced to her that there would be no abrupt endings here. Laura had also previously talked about not liking surprises. I knew we had much to explore in how we ended this therapeutic relationship. She set for herself a deadline (still wanting to be "done") but we agreed that it was flexible. I also knew that reactions would only come when she thought she was near her last (perceived) session. An image then came to me that had a profound effect on her. I described this grieving, this pain and sorrow, as being like a cape or a jacket: it's always there, but you can hang it on the peg, it doesn't always have to envelop you.

For the next three months (as the ending date changed a few times), Laura explored her feelings about leaving as well as other life issues which suddenly seemed to pop up. She began having vivid dreams: about her mother, me, escalators, elevators, falling, bombs from airplanes. The dream with me was easy for her to interpret. I was sitting next to her on the couch and she wanted to know how I felt about ending therapy. In reality, Laura never got to know how her mother felt about dying, nor did she get to tell her mother her feelings. I helped her take in that I cared about her and that our work together was meaningful to me (more than she knew), but she still felt like there was a big empty hole and didn't want to be made a fool of. In our last several sessions, I gently pushed her to explore connection and disconnection, what happens when someone is here and then not here (what is death to a ten-year-old?), and how I will still exist for her even after her last session. She cried a lot but was resolute that she wanted to end, and did.

A month and a half after our last session there was a major earthquake in the area, and Laura called within the week to say that she'd been really troubled since the earthquake and just needed to come in to talk about her feelings because she didn't feel that she could talk with Deanna about them. We had one session and we reinforced that, of course, she could talk with Deanna about her fears and anxiety. She subsequently did so, and didn't return for more sessions. I've always wondered if there had not been that particular crisis which gave Laura permission to "check in with me" (in part, I think, to see if I still existed), whether she would have called for some other reason to touch base. In any event, I feel that we accomplished so much together during the two years of work. On her last official session she gave me a framed drawing which she had commissioned, simple yet dramatic: a coat rack, with a handsome jacket hanging on one of the pegs.

REFERENCES

Brener, Anne. (1993). *Mourning & mitzvah: A guided journal for walking the mourner's path through grief to healing.* Woodstock, Vermont: Jewish Lights Publishing.

Edelman, Hope. (1994). *Motherless daughters: The legacy of loss.* New York: Addison Wesley.

Grollman, Earl. (1990). *Talking about death: A dialogue between parent and child.* Boston: Beacon Press.

Vozenilek, Helen (Ed.). (1992). *Loss of the ground-note: Women writing about the loss of their mothers.* Los Angeles: Clothespin Fever Press.

Overcoming My Model of Goodness as a Psychotherapist: Setting Boundaries— The Case of Tina

Stephanie Bot

SUMMARY. The case of Tina is presented to examine one thera-pist's countertransference issues with a female client who had fea-tures of a Borderline Personality Disorder. The therapist's emotional reactions to this client's raw expression of anger and frustration are explored. The discussion also emphasizes the struggle of the thera-pist in resolving her discomfort with this client and in setting thera-peutic boundaries. *[Article copies available for a fee from The Haworth Document Delivery Service: 1-800-342-9678. E-mail address: getinfo@ haworth.com]*

We teach what we need to learn.

—Gloria Steinem

Stephanie Bot, BA, Dip. CS, is in the process of completing her doctorate of psychology at the Adler School of Professional Psychology with a specialization in women's issues.

Address correspondence to: Stephanie Bot, 50 Holly Street, #313, Toronto, Ontario, M4S-2E9, Canada.

[Haworth co-indexing entry note]: "Overcoming My Model of Goodness as a Psychotherapist: Setting Boundaries–The Case of Tina." Bot, Stephanie. Co-published simultaneously in *Women & Therapy* (The Haworth Press, Inc.) Vol. 20, No. 1, 1997, pp. 127-130; and: *More than a Mirror: How Clients Influence Therapists' Lives* (ed: Marcia Hill) Harrington Park Press, an imprint of The Haworth Press, Inc., 1997, pp. 127-130. Single or multiple copies of this article are available for a fee from The Haworth Document Delivery Service [1-800-342-9678, 9:00 a.m. - 5:00 p.m. (EST). E-mail address: getinfo@haworth.com].

I have been providing individual and group psychotherapy for women for over three years. My specialties are in the areas of assertiveness training and self-esteem counselling. Naturally, I find myself struggling with those same issues and more recently I have become aware of how I am challenged in those areas by my own clients.

I have always identified myself as a feminist and tried to challenge the status quo. Nevertheless, I realize that instilled in my psyche is a "model of goodness" that interferes with my ability to set limits and causes me to experience tremendous guilt when I do. I suffer from the assumption, like many women, that my self-assertion will result in harming others; an outcome extremely ego-dystonic for women who believe they should be selfless.

Initially, the clients I was working with appeared to be accountable to their own "models of goodness." They were typically very polite middle-class white women, similar to myself, who were grateful for my services and careful not to overstep therapeutic boundaries with respect to time constraints and payment.

In these therapy sessions, we would all be very pleasant with one another enabling us to uphold our "models of goodness." Of course, we would discuss anger and believe we were getting to the bottom of things simply by being able to say "I felt angry when. . . ." Yet, no one ever yelled or exposed that "darker side" that would be considered unfeminine. We would role play assertiveness skills and even practice just saying the word "no." Yet I realize now that we were able to do all this while still maintaining our traditionally feminine dispositions.

Six months ago, a woman named Tina came to my office. She presented as completely different from all the other women I had been working with. Tina was angry and she was able to express her rage, while I was uncomfortable listening to it and unsure of how to respond. I thought I had been encouraging the women I worked with to explore the range of their emotions but Tina made me aware that I was only able to do this as long as their anger conformed to what I felt was "appropriate behavior." I realize now that I was limiting the women I worked with by my own limitations.

Tina challenged me in many other ways as well. She was often late for her appointments or would cancel at the last minute. She frequently forgot her money to pay for her sessions. She also usually became quite upset towards the end of her appointments, making it difficult for me to close the sessions on time. I had been teaching other women how to assert themselves in various areas of their lives and here I was struggling to set my own boundaries. I worried that I would offend Tina or that I would not meet her needs.

Nevertheless, there was a diagnosis I could consider to rationalize the problems I was confronting with Tina and ultimately take the responsibility off myself. Tina's erratic behaviors and intensity of emotion were suggestive of a diagnosis of features of a Borderline Personality Disorder. Moreover, during my training and experience, I was well-informed by the professionals I worked with that "Borderlines" were extremely challenging clients, if not impossible to treat.

Upon more thoughtful consideration around traits of a Borderline Personality Disorder, I pondered whether Tina was simply able to express what I am afraid to. Do not most women experience intense rage and frustration around issues of separation and closeness in a society that values autonomy and pathologizes dependency? Perhaps we have simply learned to repress our feelings out of fear of the repercussions to our relationships if we expressed these intense emotions.

How many times had I left my own therapist's office angry that the session was terminated just as I was getting into something I believed was important? How many times had I contained my anger when feelings of abandonment arose? For me it is a well hidden secret. Tina lets the anguish be known.

Through my reflection I could appreciate the depth of Tina's emotions and empathize with her. Prior to my introspection, however, in sessions I experienced her rage as intimidating. Moreover, her tears did not evoke my compassion as those of my other clients but rather repulsed me at times. I often felt angry at her for not conforming to more moderated behavior that I could tolerate better.

Even discussing these countertransference experiences elicits guilt in me since in my mind a "good therapist" would not feel repulsed by her client. I would have liked to refer Tina to another therapist but I felt that I would have been giving up on her and me; not to mention that I would have been playing out her abandonment issues that she was likely unconsciously setting me up for.

Rationally, I knew that I would not be helping her by enabling her to continue testing my limits. Emotionally, however, I felt guilty about not giving in to her demands. I forced myself to confront Tina with the dynamics of our relationship and to be consistent in setting boundaries. I forced myself to allow Tina to explore the range of her emotions. Although I often would squirm inside, I tried to recognize these feelings as my discomfort with my own anger and neediness rather than as Tina's "inappropriate behavior."

My experience in working with Tina has impacted on the therapy I provide to other clients as well. Since my awareness has been heightened with respect to my difficulty with intense emotions, I have become acutely sensitive to where I might be shutting off the feelings of the clients who do not openly express rage. I try to go deeper now and when I stop I ask myself why I stopped there.

Of course, my need at this point in the article is to end on a pleasant note and try to make everything nice but the truth is that after six months of therapy, Tina continues to be a challenging client.

Mandatory Reporting
and Professional Dilemmas:
A Case Study

Josephine C. H. Tan

SUMMARY. Mandatory reporting of suspicions of abuse on minors carries some risk to professional confidence in certain instances. This is of particular importance when a trainee is involved. A clinical case is described to illustrate the issues that an intern may face with respect to therapeutic alliance and professional development when reporting occurs. The issue of countertransference to reported families and its successful resolution is one that would be helpful to address in both graduate and clinical training. *[Article copies available for a fee from The Haworth Document Delivery Service: 1-800-342-9678. E-mail address: getinfo@haworth.com]*

In the practice of clinical psychology, the well-being of the client is a primary consideration. Indeed the ethical principles (APA, 1992) emphasize the therapist's responsibility for the protection of the client in all areas of professional practice. In part, this calls for the therapist to be sensitive to countertransference issues and to resolve them. Translated into practical

Josephine C. H. Tan, PhD, is currently a clinical psychologist and Assistant Professor at Lakehead University. Her interests are in the areas of depression and women's studies.

Address correspondence to: Josephine Tan, Department of Psychology, Lakehead University, Thunder Bay, Ontario, P7B 5E1, Canada.

[Haworth co-indexing entry note]: "Mandatory Reporting and Professional Dilemmas: A Case Study." Tan, Josephine C. H. Co-published simultaneously in *Women & Therapy* (The Haworth Press, Inc.) Vol. 20, No. 1, 1997, pp. 131-135; and: *More than a Mirror: How Clients Influence Therapists' Lives* (ed: Marcia Hill) Harrington Park Press, an imprint of The Haworth Press, Inc., 1997, pp. 131-135. Single or multiple copies of this article are available for a fee from The Haworth Document Delivery Service [1-800-342-9678, 9:00 a.m. - 5:00 p.m. (EST). E-mail address: getinfo@haworth.com].

terms, it is required that the therapist have considerable tolerance for anger from the client as well as the ability to carry out a certain amount of self-monitoring, self-analysis and self-control to ensure that countertransference does not interfere with the professional relationship with the client (Kleinke, 1994). Although this skill is an important factor in clinical work, it has not received much focus especially in graduate school. The negative impact of countertransference on the professional development of a young intern can be considerable. The risk, however, can be overcome with the support and consultation from the supervisor. This paper bears on this point by presenting a particularly difficult case that I encountered during my post-doctoral training. All names below are pseudonyms to protect the identity of the people involved.

The case in question involved a 13-year-old girl, Arlene Y, who was referred by a psychiatrist for diagnostic assessment. He wondered about her having multiple personality disorder as there were concerns over her oppositional and noncompliant behavior, sudden and unpredictable mood changes, memory losses, very dramatic and unexplained inappropriate behavior. She had made two relatively mild suicide attempts in the past few years, and recanted an allegation of physical abuse she had made against her mother. Arlene alternated between living in two households, one with her mother (Mrs. X) who was pregnant, stepfather, and younger brother, and the other with her father, Mr. Y.

During the course of the assessment, Arlene stated that she felt uncomfortable about her father touching and holding her, noting that sometimes she was hurt by a pen in his pocket, but would not deliver details. Her mother had also indicated in a separate session that she had often wondered about possibly inappropriate behaviour on her ex-husband's part as her daughter had spoken about receiving chest rubs from him.

At that point in time, I became very troubled. My duty to report was clear, but there were conflicting issues to be considered. I worried about the veracity of my suspicions, even though I realized that it was not my duty to verify them. I worried about the consequences to the relationships among Arlene and her family members. I worried about the "right procedure" to make a report, not having done one before.

Nevertheless, keeping in mind my duty to protect, I proceeded to remind Mrs. X about the limits of confidentiality we had covered prior to the commencement of the assessment and the need to protect her daughter. I invited her to make a report to CAS (Children's Aid Society) within 24 hours, hoping that her participation would alleviate any sense of powerlessness over the process. I noted that after that time, I would follow up with a call to CAS, and would make a report myself if she had not already done so. Although Mrs. X was upset, she indicated that she would do the reporting herself as she had concerns about her daughter's safety.

That night, I struggled with my decision to report. I reran the entire case and happenings of the day in my head several times over, wondering whether I had done the right thing. I realized, too, that I was not at all looking forward to making a report should Mrs. X fail to do so. Again and again, I wondered about the veracity of my suspicions.

The next day, I contacted Mrs. X. She had not called CAS, and attempted to dissuade me from doing so by minimizing her daughter's accounts and denying her own suspicions. When she could not bring me to ally with her, she became extremely angry and abusive. She accused me of breaking up her family. I kept an outward calm, attempting to remain gentle and sympathetic, yet appealing to the need to have our suspicions checked out by the authorities for the sake of the daughter. On the inside, however, I was torn between my wish to be empathic to her fears and concerns on one hand, and on the other my anger at what I perceived to be her unfairness and unreasonableness, and my dread at having to report. That same day, after further consultation with my supervisor and the referring psychiatrist, I contacted CAS.

For a few days thereafter, I heard nothing from Arlene, her family or CAS. That period heightened my anxiety and escalated my internal fight with the principles of clinical psychology. I intellectually recognized the need for the therapist to tolerate the client's anger in order to preserve the therapeutic alliance and well-being of the client. Yet I could not help but resent the clinical expectation that I tolerate as much as I could from clients and their families while controlling the expression of my own emotions. I repeatedly asked myself–the therapist looks after the client, but who looks after the therapist? My belief that a psychologist is like a priest, ever giving and sacrificing while asking for nothing in return, was becoming increasingly strong. I questioned my suitability to be a psychologist and entertained the idea of changing professions.

I consulted with my supervisor and the referring psychiatrist over my fears about the reporting and its consequences on Arlene and her family, and on my own professional development. Both of them were supportive and reassuring. Despite their attempts to help repair my professional confidence, I continued with my internal questions about whether psychology was asking too much of its therapists.

Several days later, a CAS worker called to inform me that they had closed the investigation because Arlene had denied any form of inappropriate behavior on the part of her father. I called Mrs. X to follow up. She stated that she held me responsible for the incident and its conse-

quences: Arlene's relationship with her father had deteriorated, her husband had hepatitis and was admitted to the hospital, and she herself (Mrs.
X) had a miscarriage and was currently suffering from depression.

Arlene's father also called to set an appointment about my reporting. He
met with my supervisor, the referring psychiatrist and myself. In the meeting, which lasted about an hour, he was furious and extremely defensive as
he expressed his rage against my female supervisor and myself and called
us incompetents, among other things. At the same time, he attempted to
ally himself with the male psychiatrist. However, both my supervisor and
the psychiatrist stood firmly by me and gently but unsuccessfully tried to
explain to him the need to protect the client. I sat on my chair the whole
time, maintaining a calm and professional mask. On the inside, I felt angry
and defenseless. My frustration was based on feeling caught between a
rock and a hard place. The two available options, to report or not to report,
held serious negative consequences for Arlene, her family and myself.

I completed my assessment report. A female therapist was assigned to
work individually with Arlene. For a while, I remained wounded and
angry at my profession. Then one day, Arlene's therapist saw me in the
corridor and drew me to one side. She whispered just one sentence, "Arlene wanted you to know that she was glad that one person believed in
her," and walked away. There and then, I felt uplifted. My actions and
pain had not been for naught. Possibly, Arlene may have derived some
benefit out of them.

To this day, I still look back at this case, and wonder how many trainees
are facing ethical dilemmas that could hurt their professional identity and
confidence. Graduate training often does not deal with the issue of countertransference, its resolution and its implications for professional development. Clinical training often does not focus on it either, as a rule, unless
the supervisor has a psychodynamic inclination as did mine.

I learned that the support of a supervisor can be very crucial. S/he not
only trains the intern for specific skills, but helps to nurture the budding
professional and develop the professional identity and confidence. During
the difficult time I had with the reporting, my supervisor was always
available and empathic, as was the referring psychiatrist for consultation.
The most stressful incident was facing Mr. Y's anger while not being able
to argue my point of view. However, the fact that my supervisor and the
referring psychiatrist stood by me and supported me made a big difference: it allowed me to work through my professional dilemmas with no
lasting damage to my professional identity and confidence.

Discussions with other clinical supervisors that I have had point to the
need for the therapist to take care of him/herself first before s/he can help

others, and to seek consultation and peer support when the need arises. However, my experience with several other clients ably demonstrates that therapeutic alliance is strengthened considerably when one is able to tolerate a client's anger, hostility and other negative states. Hence, it seems that a therapist has to control and not allow his/her own reactions to derail the therapeutic process. From this perspective, it seems reasonable for the profession of psychology to ask for such tolerance from its therapists. From another perspective, it may be potentially damaging to budding psychologists and to the discipline of clinical psychology itself when the clinical training focuses solely on skills and ignores the experiential aspects of therapy. While this issue is of relevance to the training of both male and female interns, female interns may find themselves to be in a more vulnerable position. Because of the emphasis on the nurturing aspect in their sex role socialization, women could potentially have a more difficult time accepting and resolving their negative feelings towards hostile clients.

Today, I am a clinical supervisor myself. Although I am a cognitive-behaviorist in orientation, I focus equally on the contents and process of therapy, and I discuss with my supervisee her experience as a therapist, just as my supervisors did with me. My struggle with how much of myself I should give to my clients and how much I should keep for myself is an ongoing one, and probably will remain for long time. However, my professional commitment is strong, thanks to several other clients who have provided me with positive therapy experiences.

REFERENCES

American Psychological Association (1992). Ethical principles of psychologists and code of conduct. *American Psychologist, 47*(12), 1597-1611.

Kleinke, C. L. (1994). *Common principles of psychotherapy.* Pacific Grove, California: Brooks/Cole Publishing Co.

Changes:
The Personal Consequences
of the Practice of Psychotherapy

Marcia Hill

SUMMARY. Working as a psychotherapist gradually changes the person of the therapist. The author describes the positive and negative ways she has been affected characterologically by the experience of doing therapy over many years. *[Article copies available for a fee from The Haworth Document Delivery Service: 1-800-342-9678. E-mail address: getinfo@haworth.com]*

Something over 22 years ago now, I started working as a therapist. This means I've been doing therapy for virtually all of my adult life; it's how I've spent a sizable percentage of my waking hours. I've worked with literally hundreds of people, some for just a few sessions, some for years. Hundreds of lives: a thousand secrets; ten thousand moments of intimacy, of shared anguish and laughter and the tender surprise of transformation.

Doing therapy changes a person. This should not come as news, I suppose, except that I have rarely heard others mention it. Any job done at length affects one by the simple expedient of practice. The lawyer be-

Marcia Hill, EdD, is a psychologist in private practice in Montpelier, VT, and Co-Editor of *Women & Therapy.*

Address correspondence to: Marcia Hill, 25 Court Street, Montpelier, VT 05602.

[Haworth co-indexing entry note]: "Changes: The Personal Consequences of the Practice of Psychotherapy." Hill, Marcia. Co-published simultaneously in *Women & Therapy* (The Haworth Press, Inc.) Vol. 20, No. 1, 1997, pp. 137-140; and: *More than a Mirror: How Clients Influence Therapists' Lives* (ed: Marcia Hill) Harrington Park Press, an imprint of The Haworth Press, Inc., 1997, pp. 137-140. Single or multiple copies of this article are available for a fee from The Haworth Document Delivery Service [1-800-342-9678, 9:00 a.m. - 5:00 p.m. (EST). E-mail address: getinfo@haworth.com].

comes more analytical and perhaps argumentative; the professor, didactic. I, like other therapists, I assume, have gotten more intuitive, with an impulse to help which can become intrusive if I'm not careful. And I'm clearly more skilled at intimacy than I used to be. After all, I've been in training, so to speak, for a couple of decades. I feel at home with closeness. I understand how to create it. As a side effect of one's job, this seems to me to be enormously more useful than, say, skill at computer repair or office management.

When I was a child my father delivered newspapers as a second job. I sometimes went with him and quickly came to notice newspaper boxes wherever I went. Now, years later, they're no longer salient, and I don't "see" them any more. I'm sure that the clothing designer sees the cut of a garment, whether she's working or not, in a way that I never notice. Even when "off duty," I see human distress, recognize who's depressed, notice how people treat one another.

What's more compelling, however, are not the changes that can be attributed to habit and practice, but those that are instead a consequence of knowing. By this, I mean the knowing that comes with a particular kind of lived experience, that in-the-bones knowing that changes the substance of who you are. I am reminded of the Adam and Eve story in the Bible: once you eat of the tree of the knowledge of good and evil, your life is changed utterly. What follows is a description of some of those changes.

Only in the past few years has there been some writing about "vicarious traumatization," the secondary trauma experienced by the helping person who bears witness to the stories of others' abuse. While I don't consider myself vicariously traumatized, I do know that I have not been immune to hearing people describe their pain. I am acutely sensitized to the reality of how people inflict hurt on others, to how relationships are a medium through which the damage one person bears is passed to another, most often parent to child. Most parents do better with their children than anyone who truly knows them would expect, but it seems virtually impossible not to bequeath at least a residue of hurt and confusion to the child. And pain is transmitted as well between partners, coworkers, friends.

In the telling, that pain is also passed to me. I'm well protected, of course, by the nature of my relationship with my clients. But I have learned a great deal about cruelty, intentional or not; about heartbreaking loss that can never be fully comforted; about the fundamental sorrow of life and the essential careless inhumanness of human beings. I rarely watch movies or TV shows that could be characterized as drama; they just feel like more work, and I am weighted down by the drama already present in my life. I watch sitcoms: they're resolved in half an hour and I may even get a chuckle. I garden, which is a way of reinforcing hope. I sense that my capacity to contain and attest to suffering is unnaturally enlarged. I know that this costs me in some way, but I don't yet fully know how. I imagine my heart in my chest worn down like a stair tread walked on for generations.

But doing therapy is also like watching spring come every year for several lifetimes. Just as inevitably, person after person opens into herself, comes unlocked from the cramping confinement of history and habit, shines with clarity and power. I have watched innumerable acts of courage, and have learned that when it counts the most, my integrity and emotional reliability matter far more than any skill or technique I can contribute. It is equally obvious to me that while my participation is occasionally crucial and usually helpful to what happens, the magic that occurs in therapy is by no means the creation of the therapist. In the end, the possibility and direction of change belong to the other person.

I do not mean in any way to undervalue what I, or other therapists, do. After all, if the person were able to get untangled himself, it is unlikely he would have arrived at my door. I am quite aware of my role as alchemist, daily handling the power to transmute. Nonetheless, there is an organic process at work here, some impulse toward completion and well-being, that is the real agent of transformation.

How can I witness miracles and not be affected? In my own life, I have the great fortune thus to know how to assist my own transformation. I trust unequivocally the human capacity for resolution, regardless of how dark the way appears. When I experienced a major loss some time ago, I had no reason to fear my sometimes excruciating grief: I knew absolutely that the psyche has the capacity to heal even what feels impossibly destroyed. I have watched with humbled amazement as people, many people, not just the rare exception, did what I knew to be the hardest work of their lives. And so I know that if humans can be limited and self-absorbed, they are also unarguably brave and loving and full of honor. The work of therapy is spiritual work, in that it rides on the wings of the ineffable. That lifts me as well.

Intimate acquaintance with so many lives offers a window on the multitude of ways that people live, both practically and psychologically. People are endlessly inventive, and one of the benefits of being a therapist is that you don't have to live locked in the limitations of your own perspective. For myself, this has meant a kind of compassionate softening, a recognition that there are many solutions to the dilemma of being alive and that "human nature" is as various as human appearance. I am privileged to have some sense of the range of what is normal, in the sense of workable as well as frequent. That knowledge is comforting. Being a therapist tends to create tolerance, and it's a small step from there to self-acceptance.

And so, most important is the change that comes, unexpected, as a summary of all these elements. If therapists are exposed to what is most tragic in life, we are also privy to what is most inspiring. We have the benefit of experiencing many lives. If we are paying any attention at all, we have the possibility of developing wisdom.

Index

AA (Alcoholics Anonymous),
17,18,19,20
Accommodation, 104,106
African Americans, therapeutic
relationships of, 5-14
AIDS (acquired immune deficiency
syndrome) patients, 51-56
family of, 54-55
friends of, 53-54
Alanon, 17
Alcoholic clients, 15,16-20
enabling of, 17-19
Alcoholics Anonymous (AA),
17,18,19,20
Alternative Family Project, 58-59
Altruism, 16
Amnesty International, 36
Anger, of clients, 95
Arousal
intrusive memories-related, 103
sexual versus nonsexual, 69-71
Assertiveness training, 128
Assimilation, 104
Avoidance behaviors, as traumatic
memory response, 103-104

Bereavement. *See also* Mourning
experienced by client, 30-31
experienced by therapist,
29-30,31
as therapist-client parallel
process, 119-126
Borderline personality disorder
patients,
countertransference with,
127-130
Burnout, experienced by trauma
therapists, 102

Canada
marginalization in, 85
multiculturalism in, 87-88,90
Vietnamese refugees in, 85-87
Catharsis, 16
Change, elements required for, 16
Cheerfulness, excessive emphasis on,
45-48
Children
abuse of
deaths caused by, 39-44
sexual, mandatory reporting
of, 32,131-135
as clients
Native-American, 1-4
sexual abuse of, 31-32,
131-132
therapeutic needs of, 1-4
mother's murder of, 39-44
Clients
anger of, 95
borderline personality disorder,
127-130
children as
Native-American, 1-4
sexual abuse of, 31-32,
131-132
therapeutic needs of, 1-4
male
misogynistic, 111-117
provider role of, 98-99
of racialized therapists, 88-89,
90
therapeutic relationship with,
97-100
merger with, 91-96
pregnancy of, 37-38,73-76
therapist's protection of, 131-132
torture victims as, 23-25,36

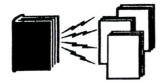

Haworth
DOCUMENT DELIVERY
SERVICE

This valuable service provides a single-article order form for any article from a Haworth journal.

- *Time Saving:* No running around from library to library to find a specific article.
- *Cost Effective:* All costs are kept down to a minimum.
- *Fast Delivery:* Choose from several options, including same-day FAX.
- *No Copyright Hassles:* You will be supplied by the original publisher.
- *Easy Payment:* Choose from several easy payment methods.

Open Accounts Welcome for . . .
- Library Interlibrary Loan Departments
- Library Network/Consortia Wishing to Provide Single-Article Services
- Indexing/Abstracting Services with Single Article Provision Services
- Document Provision Brokers and Freelance Information Service Providers

---

MAIL or *FAX* THIS ENTIRE ORDER FORM TO:

Haworth Document Delivery Service
The Haworth Press, Inc.
10 Alice Street
Binghamton, NY 13904-1580

or FAX: 1-800-895-0582
or CALL: 1-800-342-9678
9am-5pm EST

PLEASE SEND ME PHOTOCOPIES OF THE FOLLOWING SINGLE ARTICLES:

1) Journal Title: _____

   Vol/Issue/Year:_____Starting & Ending Pages:_____

Article Title:_____

_____

2) Journal Title: _____

   Vol/Issue/Year:_____Starting & Ending Pages:_____

Article Title:_____

_____

3) Journal Title: _____

   Vol/Issue/Year:_____Starting & Ending Pages:_____

Article Title:_____

_____

4) Journal Title: _____

   Vol/Issue/Year:_____Starting & Ending Pages:_____

Article Title:_____

_____

(See other side for Costs and Payment Information)

COSTS: Please figure your cost to order quality copies of an article.

1. Set-up charge per article: $8.00
   ($8.00 × number of separate articles) _____

2. Photocopying charge for each article:

   1-10 pages: $1.00 _____

   11-19 pages: $3.00 _____

   20-29 pages: $5.00 _____

   30+ pages: $2.00/10 pages _____

3. Flexicover (optional): $2.00/article _____

4. Postage & Handling: US: $1.00 for the first article/
   $.50 each additional article _____

   Federal Express: $25.00 _____

   Outside US: $2.00 for first article/
   $.50 each additional article _____

5. Same-day FAX service: $.35 per page _____

GRAND TOTAL: _____

METHOD OF PAYMENT: (please check one)

❑ Check enclosed   ❑ Please ship and bill. PO # _____
(sorry we can ship and bill to bookstores only! All others must pre-pay)

❑ Charge to my credit card: ❑ Visa; ❑ MasterCard; ❑ Discover;
❑ American Express;

Account Number: _____ Expiration date: _____

Signature: ✗ _____

Name: _____ Institution: _____

Address: _____

_____

City: _____ State: _____ Zip: _____

Phone Number: _____ FAX Number: _____

MAIL or *FAX* THIS ENTIRE ORDER FORM TO:

Haworth Document Delivery Service
The Haworth Press, Inc.
10 Alice Street
Binghamton, NY 13904-1580

or FAX: 1-800-895-0582
or CALL: 1-800-342-9678
9am-5pm EST)